THE REBIRTH OF THE LAITY

THE
REBIRTH
OF THE LAITY

HOWARD GRIMES

ABINGDON PRESS
NEW YORK • NASHVILLE

THE REBIRTH OF THE LAITY

Copyright © 1962 by Abingdon Press

Library of Congress Catalog Card Number: 62-16810

SET UP, PRINTED, AND BOUND BY THE
PARTHENON PRESS, AT NASHVILLE,
TENNESSEE, UNITED STATES OF AMERICA

In gratitude to my mother and father
devoted laymen in the church

PREFACE

The central concern of this book is the Church, though it is not in any exact sense a theology of the Church. It deals with a particular emphasis—the Church as the whole people of God, or, in other words, with the laity. This does not mean that it is not also concerned with the clergy, for the two cannot be separated. The major emphasis, however, is on those members of the Body of Christ who are not engaged in "set-apart" ministries.

I first became interested in this subject some years ago when I was engaged in a historical study of the training of laymen for leadership in The Methodist Church. This study engaged me in a consideration of the *meaning* of the laity, although very little contemporary writing had been done in the field at that time. To be sure, pioneer work was already under way under the auspices of the World Council of Churches, and this has continued to be one of the major sources of help since that time.

Some years later, as I worked on what was to have been a revision of the dissertation which resulted from the original study, I was pushed back still another step to a consideration of the nature and mission of the Church. This led, in 1958, to *The Church Redemptive*. Since then I have done further historical study on the laity in America, participating in a consultation on "The Laity in Historical Perspective" under the auspices of the Department of the Laity of the World Council of Churches in 1959. I had previously been privileged to visit many of the "lay centers" which have emerged in

7

Europe primarily since World War II; and then, during the summer of 1961, I attended the *Kirchentag* in West Berlin and made additional contacts with leaders of the lay institutes.

I am greatly indebted to the leaders of the institutes, to those who participated in the consultation at Bossey, and to various writers who have considered this subject during recent years. I have also utilized information provided by a number of people concerning what is happening in the United States, and unfortunately many of these people remain unnamed. I am especially grateful to Hendrik Kraemer and Arnold Come for their discussions of the laity, and to Franklin Littell and Margaret Frakes for their discussions of the lay centers. My indebtedness to many others is indicated in the footnotes.

I am also grateful for the help of Mrs. Anne Norris and Mrs. Dorothy Laughbaum who assisted in the preparation of the manuscript.

Although there is now nothing new about the approach to the laity which is formulated in this book, the point of view is far from being implemented. I have therefore tried to indicate ways in which it is being carried out in various situations and to make further suggestions which I hope will be of help to those who are involved in the life of the Church. My emphases betray the fact that I am convinced that part of the answer lies in more adequate adult education in the Church.

Although these pages are addressed to both clergy and laity, it is the laity which must in the final analysis be responsible for the new lay emphasis by their commitment to and understanding of the Christian gospel. Or, to put it more exactly, the rebirth of the laity can occur only as laymen allow themselves to be used of God for the renewal of the Church.

HOWARD GRIMES

CONTENTS

CHAPTER 1

INTRODUCTION

This is a book *about* and partly *for* the laity, though it is hoped that the clergy will also take its point of view seriously. That is, it is primarily concerned with those members of the Church who have not been set apart for special full-time functions in the Church. It deals with the ministry of the Church, but not alone with those who serve the Church in set-apart positions. It seeks to describe in both theory and practice how the *total* ministry may be exercised in the twentieth-century world.

The use of the word "laity" to denote these nonprofessional members of the Church's ministry is considered by some as a misuse of the term, for the various forms of the word "lay" come from the Greek word *laos*, which ordinarily means the whole people. Thus *ho laos tou Theou*, as applied to the Church, means "the people of God." In this sense all persons who have been called into the Body of Christ are *laos* (people, laymen), a people called of God to be his special agency in the world. Since some term must be used to designate the unordained members of the Church, however, and since this term goes back as far as the late first century, "lay," "laymen," "laity" will be used throughout these chapters in that respect. When special attention must be called to the sex of these lay members, *laywomen* will be used, and this must be done on

11

occasion since the Church has not always taken seriously Paul's statement that there is neither male nor female in Christ Jesus (Gal. 3:28). Generally, however, layman is used without discrimination.

This is of necessity also a book about the Church. As both a Roman Catholic[1] and a Protestant[2] have recently insisted, it is impossible to talk about lay people in the Church without expressing or implying a doctrine of the Church. As a matter of fact, it is necessary to put the discussion in the setting of a total biblical theology which, though brief, provides meaningful background.

Further, we must be aware of the world in which the Church is set and in which the laity live their lives. The Church neither can nor ought to be an agency set apart from the world, to be kept away from the exigencies of the common life. There are religious groups which try to do this, and there are both clergy and laity in all churches who would like to disassociate the Church and its message from all concern with business, economic life, political decisions, and world affairs. The very nature of the Church, its gospel, and its mission make such a point of view untenable. The gospel, as Jesus was clear in saying, demands a total response which touches all areas of life. "You are the salt of the earth . . . the light of the world" is one way of putting this.[3] If the organized church cannot lead its membership to speak and act creatively and Christianly in such areas as race relations, economic justice, disarmament, world affairs, the abuse of alcohol, the threats to freedom of speech, and similar matters, then it is failing in its mission to the world as the carrier of the gospel of Jesus Christ.

It is especially evident in a discussion of the laity that it is impossible to ignore the world (that is, society, culture, political institutions, economic life, and the like) in which the Church is set. The clergy to some extent are protected from the world (rather too much, some would insist). The major

12

portion of the time of most clergymen is spent either directly or indirectly in doing the special work of the Church, or in some more or less official relationship with other clergymen and laymen in the name of the organized church. Although he by no means avoids the pervasive influence of the culture of which he is a part,[4] his decisions are somewhat less directly related to the daily round of life than those of the layman.[5]

The layman is not subject to this amount of freedom from the world. How he makes his living—unless he is employed by a church—is the most obvious point of contact with the culture. It is only one, however, for his total life, except for those few hours spent in worship, Christian education, and church visitation or as a choir member, committee member, or church official, is lived outside the confines of the organized church. So influential is the culture in which he lives that it is often only through conscious and difficult thinking that his decisions can be made apart from cultural influences.

If we were living in a stable society whose norms and values were determined by the Christian faith, our problem would be a different one.[6] Although we cannot deny that to some extent American life is still governed by values derived from the Judaeo-Christian tradition, there is an increasing weight of evidence that there is far less of this than we at times optimistically surmise. Modern man, we are told incessantly, is involved in a world of ideas and forces congenial neither to stability of life nor to an easy expression of the Christian faith. It is not primarily the preachers who remind us of this fact; indeed, some observers would insist that modern sermons tend to assume rather too much about the Christian quality of our culture. To be sure, perceptive theologians such as Reinhold Niebuhr and Paul Tillich point to the reality of our sub-Christian culture, but it is in the arts that we discern most fully man's sickness. Dramatists such as Tennessee Williams and Arthur Miller, essayists such as William H. Whyte, Jr., David Riesman, and Vance Packard, and novelists such as

13

William Faulkner, Albert Camus, and Jack Kerouac combine to paint a picture of sin more vivid than that found in Paul's Letter to the Romans.

How many of our problems are caused and how many others are aggravated by the insecurity of a world which stands under the threat of nuclear destruction it is impossible to say; nor is it easy to assess how much a factor in our problems is the rapidly changing character of our world. Such conditions are in themselves sufficient to cause deep distress in the mind of man; unfortunately they have come at a time when the moorings of both the individual and society are deeply affected by conscious and unconscious questions concerning the meaning of life. Even the churches have been affected by these forces so that they are less able to cope with the searchings of modern man than they ought to be. When individual man as well as society is being shaken by world catastrophes and revolutions in thought and action, the Church has too often offered palliatives for the alleviation of immediate symptoms of insecurity and doubt rather than clearly proclaiming the kind of faith which can provide the foundations on which can be built a more adequate life.

Since there is no consensus as to how these conditions ought to be described, any attempt to categorize them is likely to meet with disagreement. There are certain persistent themes which may be discerned, however, one of the more common being the meaninglessness of life for many people. J. D. Salinger has portrayed this eloquently on the teen-age level in *The Catcher in the Rye*. One of the more telling scenes during Holden Caulfield's "lost weekend" in New York City occurs in his hotel room. He has tried everything he knows to try to make something of his time, and finally in desperation he tries to pray. But this fails also. And so he says, "Finally I sat up in bed and smoked another cigarette." [7] And Camus has concluded: "Judging whether life is or is not worth living amounts to answering the fundamental question of philosophy." [8]

Part of this meaninglessness results from the depersonalization of man, which in turn has occurred partly because of the technological revolution through which we have been—and still are passing. The title of David Riesman's best-known work is more than a catchword, it is also a description of the situation of man in a highly technical society: "the lonely crowd." [9] Another way of describing this depersonalization is estrangement from life—alienation, or lostness. Man is threatened by forces over which he has no control, and his faith is not strong enough to support him when the "props" that have previously supported him are gone. In the face of such "demonic" forces, our loss of faith stands out as the underlying cause of many of the other symptoms to which we might point.

Not everyone is caught up in these conditions, to be sure, though I suspect most of us are involved to some extent. If only we would stop our feverish activity, turn off the television sets, and sit down completely alone we would probably find that we are less sure of ourselves than we like to give the outward impression of being. In any case, we should not be led to despair because of the difficulties of life. It is when man is at the end of his tether that he is most likely to turn to God. The psalmist sensed this centuries ago: those involved in a terrific storm "were at their wit's end. Then they cried to the Lord in their trouble." (Ps. 107:27b-28a.) It well may be that there is a greater opportunity for the proclamation of the deepest insights of the Christian faith than there has been for many centuries.

Unfortunately, however, at the very time that outer threats have become most critical, the churches have tended to allow the culture to affect both their lives and their message. While church statistics have steadily gone upward, the distinctiveness of the Church and its message has been blurred. As the Church has tended to become a cultural institution—or an institution of culture—it has participated in the exigencies of the society it is commanded to serve. To be sure, these

15

sweeping generalizations must be qualified, for there is much within the Church contrary to these trends. But without the recognition of these tendencies (that is, the sin of the Church), there is little hope for reform. God cannot work his miracle of grace in either the individual or the group—even the Church—except there be repentance.

The evidences for the decline of the organized church are more obvious in Europe than in America and in the northeastern part of the United States than in the Midwest. European statistics have consistently indicated that only a small portion of the population is actively related to the Church even though 99 per cent of a nation may be baptized. In America, where more than 60 per cent of the population belong to a church and where census figures indicate that a much larger percentage consider themselves in some vague way "religious," most local congregations have a substantial number of members who cannot be located at all and an even larger number whose participation in the life of the Church can be considered at best nominal. The postwar upsurge of interest in religion has apparently run its course, and the analysts of that movement are quite rightly raising questions concerning its depth. Bishop Pike's conclusions must be studied seriously; namely, that not only has a decline set in, but that the upsurge itself was without substance.[10]

Whatever the statistics may be, then, they tell only part of the story. There is an increasing amount of evidence that much of the religion which is held by Americans is something other than the Christian gospel with its message of the holy love of God which comes to man in both judgment and grace. Will Herberg has concluded that the "American Way of Life is the symbol by which Americans define themselves and establish their unity," [11] and therefore is for them in reality their religion. Although the American way of life has much in common with the Judaeo-Christian heritage in terms of basic morality, the two are not identical and the former turns out to be essentially "an idealized description of the middle-class ethos." [12] So pervasive is this culture-religion that, according to Herberg, religionists and secularists cherish "the same basic values and organize their lives on the same fundamental assumptions—values and assumptions defined by the American Way of Life." [13]

What Herberg describes is essentially what Richard Niebuhr had earlier called the "Christ of culture" motif in the relation of Christianity and culture; that is, the accommodation of the Church to culture rather than its being a critic of culture.[14] Roy Eckardt has used another term to describe the same phenomenon—"folk religion." [15] The example par excellence of folk religion is the gospel of success and peace of mind. The emphasis is on being decent, on working hard and being successful, and on "utilizing the resources of religion" in achieving both of these ends. "To the extent that God has a place in folk religion, he is fundamentally a helpmate, guide, and friend." [16]

Martin Marty has chosen still another term to denote popular religion in America—"religion-in-general." He recognizes, as we must, that this is neither historic Protestantism nor the best of Protestantism as manifest in the churches today. But, he says, we are basically living in a post-Protestant era and this religion-in-general "swirls around the churches and sometimes flourishes in them." [17] The religion which results is basically American in character, only secondarily Christian. It tends to emphasize belief in *human* values, *human* freedom, *human* achievement, and rewards for such *human* goodness.[18] Other writers such as Gibson Winter,[19] Peter Berger,[20] Claire Cox,[21] and Gerhard Lenski [22] have come to similar conclusions about the nature of American popular religion.

Although this is not the whole picture, it must not be ignored. We can be grateful that there are also signs of the working of the Holy Spirit both for the renewal of the Church and for the redemption of modern man. In the midst of both

17

the threats to the individual and the misinterpretations of the Christian faith, certain movements are occurring that may well serve as the means which God uses to renew the Church in this generation. Four of these are especially pertinent to our considerations.

First, there is the recovery of biblical theology. Two opposite factors have been at work during recent decades to obscure the meaning of the Bible. On the one hand, exponents of historical criticism of the Bible have often failed to recognize that the biblical message is not nullified by the efforts of those who seek to analyze the background, writing, and contents of the Bible. On the other hand, there have been literalists who have failed to see that the message of the Bible must be related to a particular time and place; that we cannot equate the message of the Bible with the particular scientific worldview in which it is stated; that the revelation to which the Bible points is not one of propositional statements about God but rather God's personal word to man.

Further, our understanding of the essential message of the Bible has often been hindered by a misplaced emphasis on nonessentials. Current biblical theology, including the work done by such diverse scholars as Barth and Bultmann, agrees with the historical critics with respect to the necessity of critically evaluating the form of the message of the Bible but seeks to find modern forms through which its essential message can be made relevant to man in his estrangement and anxiety.

Second, there is a rediscovery of the meaning and significance of the Church, largely a by-product of the ecumenical movement. In its fear lest it make an idol of the Church (as it felt Roman Catholicism had done), Protestantism has often failed to recognize its importance. Under the impact of Western individualism and the left wing of the Reformation, the Church tended to be thought of as a collection of individuals with no *esse* (being) of its own, an appendage to

18

Christianity. More recently churchmen have been discovering the Church as the Body of Christ.

Third, in this rethinking of the nature of the Church there is an emphasis on the meaning of the laity such as has not existed since the early decades of the Christian movement. Whereas in the past discussions of the nature of the Church were more likely to center in a consideration of the nature of the ordained ministry, now they are just as likely to be concerned with the meaning of the laity or the whole people of God. Part of this may be the result of a kind of desperation on the part of churchmen, especially in Europe, but it lies deeper than this and is based upon an understanding of the Church as *people*—the *whole* people—under God. Further, it has been increasingly recognized that its mission can be fulfilled only through the entire body of people, laity as well as clergy.

Fourth, there is a burgeoning emphasis on adult study of the Christian faith: Bible, theology, church history, ethics. The form it has most often taken in Europe in the lay study center (such as the Evangelical Academies in Germany, to be discussed later). In the United States it is more likely to be in the form of the small study group in the local parish, providing an occasion not only for study but also for a deepened fellowship (*koinonia*).

If the conditions described earlier in this chapter are to any degree true, the necessity for such study and fellowship becomes abundantly clear. Laymen, immunized by a post-Protestant and semi-Christian brand of folk religion, are unlikely to hear the radical demands of the gospel in a brief and easily ignored sermon. Some place must be found where the deepest needs of individuals may be met and where they may be met in terms of the gospel. The small fellowship-study groups appear to be the form it is most likely to take.

We shall be concerned to some extent with the first two of these signs of hope and renewal and more extensively with the last two. We now turn our attention to these.

NOTES

1. Yves M. J. Congar, *Lay People in the Church: A Study for a Theology of the Laity*, trans. Donald Attwater (Westminster, Md.: The Newman Press, 1957, 1959).
2. From *A Theology of the Laity* by Hendrik Kraemer. © Hendrik Kraemer, 1958. Published The Westminster Press 1959. By permission.
3. Matt. 5:13-16. See also Matt. 6:25-34; 19:23-30; Mark 12:28-34; Luke 10:25-37; 14:25-33; 18:18-30.
4. For evidence as to how much the clergy is affected by the "world," one need only note how much the image of the business executive has helped to form the image of the clergy. This is reflected in two recent discussions of the clergy: H. Richard Niebuhr (in collaboration with Daniel Day Williams and James M. Gustafson), *The Purpose of the Church and Its Ministry* (New York: Harper & Brothers, 1956), especially pp. 48-58; and Samuel W. Blizzard, "The Minister's Dilemma," *The Christian Century*, LXXIII (Apr. 25, 1956), 508-10.
5. This is not meant to deny that in the pastor's decisions concerning what to preach, what to say about controversial issues such as race relations and so on he is not affected by his immediate cultural context.
6. The relationship of the Church and culture is always a matter which must be taken into account, of course, as is shown in H. Richard Niebuhr's *Christ and Culture* (New York: Harper & Brothers, 1951).
7. J. D. Salinger, *The Catcher in the Rye* (a Signet Book, published by The New American Library, 1953, 1959), p. 92.
8. Albert Camus, "An Absurd Reasoning," in *The Myth of Sisyphus and Other Essays*, trans. Justin O'Brien (New York: Vintage Books, 1955), p. 3.
9. David Riesman (with Nathan Glazer and Reuel Denney), *The Lonely Crowd* (New York: Doubleday Anchor Books, 1953).
10. James A. Pike, "Christianity Is in Retreat," *Look*, December 20, 1960, p. 23. See also Martin E. Marty, *The New Shape of American Religion* (New York: Harper & Brothers, 1958, 1959), Chap. 1.
11. From *Protestant-Catholic-Jew* by Will Herberg. Copyright © 1955 by Will Herberg. Reprinted by permission of Doubleday & Co., Inc. P. 91.
12. *Ibid.*, p. 94.
13. *Ibid.*, p. 287.
14. Richard Niebuhr, *op. cit.*, Chap. 3.
15. A. Roy Eckardt, *The Surge of Piety in America* (New York: Association Press, 1958), especially Chap. 2.
16. *Ibid.*, p. 49.
17. Marty, *op. cit.*, p. 32; see also pp. 31-34.
18. *Ibid.*, Chap. 4.
19. From *The Suburban Captivity of the Churches* by Gibson Winter. Copyright © 1961 by Gibson Winter. Reprinted by permission of Doubleday & Co., Inc.
20. Peter Berger, *The Noise of Solemn Assemblies* (Garden City, N.Y.: Doubleday & Company, Inc., 1961).
21. Claire Cox, *The New-Time Religion* (Englewood Cliffs, N.J.: Prentice-Hall, Inc., 1961).
22. Gerhard Lenski, *The Religious Factor* (Garden City, N.Y.: Doubleday & Company, Inc., 1961).

20

CHAPTER 2

THE BIBLICAL SETTING

The previous chapter has described in brief the present setting in which the laity lives, along with some of the temptations to which modern American religion is subjected. One of the signs of hope which was indicated at the close of the chapter was the recovery of biblical theology. It is fitting that we look next, then, at the biblical setting for our interest in the laity. In the first place, it is the Bible which repeatedly calls the Church back to a more adequate expression of its faith, and thus the Bible stands in judgment against the religion-in-general which affects the Church today. In the second place, it is the Bible which points to the answer to man's need —not his superficial desires but the deepest and most persistent aspects of the human quandary. It is the faith of the Christian that God has acted not in a general way, that the Christian faith is not a set of general principles interpreting reality, but rather that it is God's answer to the human dilemma of meaninglessness and estrangement. Revelation—God's act—is *to* man in *man's* need.[1]

It would be presumptuous to suppose that biblical theology could be adequately summarized in a single chapter. To make such an attempt, one inevitably falls into the danger against which a New Testament scholar has recently warned; namely, the implication that there is a single, simple biblical theology.

21

Although "there is a basic unity of purpose, conviction, and concern which gives a profound integrity to the biblical witness," there is also a "rich diversity of perspective which in itself attests to the lively and very real encounter of men who meet God in the concrete circumstances of their daily pursuits." [2] That which is said in the following section is thus only an attempt to state some of the important aspects of man's encounter with God which are pertinent to our own meeting with him today, largely from the prophetic and the Pauline points of view.

A Covenant Theology [3]

Whatever else the biblical faith is, it is at least a covenant faith. God creates man for fellowship with him—"in his image" (Gen. 1:26-27). The fellowship is broken because of man's disobedience (Gen. 3:1-19).[4] God seeks to win man back through Noah, with the rainbow as the sign of the covenant with all mankind (Gen. 9:8-17).[5] God again works through Abraham, this time to call unto himself a people (Gen. 12 ff.), but the nature of the relationship is vague and only partially formed. Circumcision is the sign of this covenant (Gen. 17:9 ff.).

It is only with Moses that the covenant takes on clearer form and focus, for now a cultus begins to form around the relationship. It was ordinarily the deliverance of Israel from Egypt under Moses as the great salvation event in her history to which the prophets referred in their attempts to call Israel back to the covenant faith. (See, for example, Amos 3:1, Hos. 11:1, and Ps. 78:9-20.) The Passover as the symbol of deliverance and salvation became the sign of this covenant; and from this time forward, regardless of the misfortunes which befell them and the apostasy which characterized the people, Israel possessed a self-consciousness which was kept alive by prophet and priest. Israel was the people of Yahweh, bound to Israel by an irrevocable covenant. Even Paul, steeped as he was in the Hebrew scriptures, never quite solved the problem of the relationship of this covenant to the new, as mightily as he struggled to do so in Rom. 9-11.

Israel's faith was a covenant faith. But what is a covenant? It is basically an agreement binding two or more persons or groups, or a relationship involving mutual obligations. Bernhard Anderson,[6] with due warning for its inadequacy, has likened the covenant faith of the Bible to the marriage relationship in which two persons bind themselves together not so much on a legal basis as on the basis of commitment and trust. Now, of course, this covenant is between equals, and the covenant between God and man is between unequals. Yet both God and Israel pledge themselves to a certain agreement: God to be faithful to Israel, Israel to be faithful to Yahweh. (See especially Exod. 23:20–24:8). One writer has put this succinctly but meaningfully in these words: "God has *done something* and the relationship thus established between him and his People brings forth from them a response of faith and gratitude." [7]

It is of special importance that it was all of Israel that was called to be God's people. In Exod. 19:6 occurs this illuminating passage: "And you shall be to me a kingdom of priests and a holy nation." To be sure a special priesthood developed in Israel, and the people often lost their sense of corporate priesthood. Yet the idea persisted of the whole people as the people of God (*ho laos tou Theou*), especially in the prophets and some of the psalms. Jeremiah (13:11), Hosea (2:23), Amos (3:1-2), and Ezekiel (37:27) are among those who either restate or echo the idea.

But Israel was unfaithful to its side of the agreement! Over and over again this was the burden of the prophets. It is stated in harsh terms by Amos:

23

You only have I known
of all the families of the earth;
therefore I will punish you
for all your iniquities.

—3:2

Hosea expresses the concept more poignantly:

When Israel was a child, I loved him,
and out of Egypt I called my son.
The more I called them,
the more they went from me;
they kept sacrificing to the Baals,
and burning incense to idols.

Yet it was I who taught Ephraim to walk,
I took them up in my arms;
but they did not know that I healed them.
I led them with cords of compassion,
with the bands of love,
and I became to them as one
who eases the yoke on their jaws,
and I bent down to them and fed them.

—11:1-4

Out of the discipline of the disaster [8] of the captivity in the sixth century came new insights and new resolves. Probably even earlier the idea of a faithful remnant had developed (Isa. 10:20-33). During the captivity the understanding of suffering as a means of redemption arose, as found in the "suffering servant" passages of Second Isaiah. Israel must suffer as a means of service to the world, in order that she might become a "light to the Gentiles" and "the witness of God's glory to the whole world" [9] (see Isa. 42:1-9 and 52:13–53:12). The first of these concepts Paul applied to the Church (Rom. 9:27). The second is the chief figure by which the nature of

24

the messiahship of Jesus was understood by the early Church.

Although postexilic Judaism became increasingly nationalistic and legalistic, the prophetic note was not forgotten. One of the finest expressions of prophetic understanding, for example, is found in the prayer of Ezra, in which he recounts the whole history of God's dealing with Israel (Neh. 9:6-37). The story is one of continued faithfulness of God, of unfaithfulness of Israel. "Because of all this," the writer continues, "we make a firm covenant and write it, and our princes, our Levites, and our priests set their seal to it." (Neh. 9:38.)

But Suzanne de Dietrich's conclusion is unfortunately correct: "Thus post-exilic Judaism, with all the positive values we have already stressed, is threatened with becoming a faith imbued with nationalism on the one hand and legalism on the other." [10] It was against the narrow legalism of the Pharisees that both Jesus and Paul reacted, for though the motives of this strict sect were noble, the end result was unfortunate.

The Pharisees had "separated" from the bulk of the people in order to submit themselves to a self-imposed discipline at a time of general religious and moral decadence. They were the exponents of the strict observance of the law. But their passion for the law led many of them to a kind of fanaticism. . . . Theirs became a religion of works—demanding of themselves, merciless for others.[11]

One other important development in Judaism is of special significance for Christianity; namely, the growth of the hope that God would send a deliverer, or Messiah, to save Israel once again. The covenant which had begun on a worldwide scale with Noah had been narrowed to a people with Abraham and a cultic group with Moses. Now it was to be renewed in one faithful man, the Messiah. The Christian affirmation is that God did precisely this in Jesus of Nazareth, the Christ or the Messiah.

Jesus apparently considered his work as a continuation of

25

the work which God had done through Israel. (See, for example, Matt. 5:17-20.) Yet it was inevitable that the new wine could not be contained in the old wineskins (Matt. 9: 17). God had come into history in a unique way in Jesus Christ, and the faith which stemmed from him, as Paul clearly saw, could not remain a sect within Judaism. John the Baptist announces that the Kingdom is at hand (Matt. 3:2). A remnant awaits the coming of the Kingdom (Luke 2:25-32). And so the "New Israel" is formed from the humble poor, from the sick and the outcast, from fishermen and tax collectors who listen and follow.[12] God works his new miracle through Jesus Christ, the suffering servant, who ends the old age and inaugurates the new, putting an end to the sacrificial system of Judaism, drawing man to God by the power of his suffering love. He was, to use the terms of J. S. Whale, both victim and victor: victim of man's sin, dying to show the seriousness with which God takes that sin, but rising again as victor over sin and drawing men to the one who loves man to the uttermost, even in his sin.[13]

It is the Christian's conviction that God has done for him through Christ what he could not do for himself (atonement); that he is put in right relationship with God not by his merit but by God's goodness, grace, and forgiveness (justification); and that he responds to God's holy love by acknowledging who he is (repentance), accepting God's love (reconciliation), and living responsibly before God and his neighbor (the Christian life). But he does not live in isolation, for he has been called into the new community and he is a person in community. In other words he is a part of the total Body of Christ, the Church. Although the New Testament writers use different terms to describe this new life in Christ (John, for example, uses "eternal life"), they seem to me to be centrally concerned with what God had done in Christ and man's response to it.

From this brief summary several important conclusions may be drawn. First, it is *God who acts*, who takes the initiative.

Man may search for God, to be sure, but his search is met by God's previous action. It was God who acted in the events of history to which the prophets and others responded; and though he acts in judgment, he also acts in love. It is God who acts fully and completely in Jesus Christ. It is God (Holy Spirit) who acted in the Church in the events described in the Acts of the Apostles and who acts today in the Church. The Church is fundamentally the community of the Holy Spirit.

Second, *man is asked to respond.* There were conditions to the covenant with Moses (the keeping of the Law). There are conditions placed upon those who respond to God today, even though God's love is unconditional. The new covenant in Christ comes to man as God's free gift, but accepting the gift places upon man the obligation to act responsibly as part of the new community. As we have seen, much modern religion in America, like that to which Israel was wont to fall victim, hopes to enjoy the benefits of the covenant without its obligations.

Third, man is never completely alone before God; *he is always in community.* To be sure, both Jeremiah (31:29-34) and Ezekiel (18:1-4) foreshadowed the sense of individual worth and responsibility before God which the New Testament makes clear; and the lonely prophet standing as one against the whole community is a common figure in the Old Testament. But we must never forget that the community is assumed in the Old Testament, that the prophet went forth *from* and spoke *to* the community, assuming that the whole community—or a remnant—must stand together. Jesus gathered about him a community of disciples; and following the Resurrection, new groups of disciples very quickly began to form in cities throughout the Roman world. The sense of community (*koinonia*—partnership, participation, fellowship) is strong in the New Testament, so strong in the book of Acts,

27

for example, that the holding of goods in common was tried temporarily (Acts 4:32–5:11).

Fourth, *God does in Jesus Christ what man cannot do for himself,* calling men out of darkness into light. Man responds in faith and love to the gracious activity of God through the Holy Spirit today. He is called into the community of the Spirit, the Church, and sent into the world to live Christianly in relation to his neighbor. However far short Christians fall from this goal, this is their call.

The New Community [14]

We have said that our generation has not only recovered the importance of the biblical message but has also rediscovered the Church. Perhaps it would be impossible to do the former without the latter coming to pass, for as we have said the Bible continually emphasizes the community (holy nation, holy people) which comes into being as a result of God's call to man. The extreme religious individualism characteristic of much of Protestantism during past decades, which considers the Church as an appendage to Christianity, simply has no basis in the New Testament.

Ekklesia. The word translated "church" in the English versions of the New Testament is *ekklesia,* those who are called out and assembled together. It was originally a secular word in Greek, used in the Septuagint (the Greek translation of the Hebrew scriptures) as an equivalent for the Hebrew *Qahal,* and taken over by many of the New Testament writers as a way of describing the assembling of Christians. As Karl Ludwig Schmidt has said in his article "The Church" in Kittel's *Wordbook of the New Testament:* "The mere gathering tells us nothing; everything depends on the character of those who are gathered. . . . The essential is that God gathers his own." And later, "The one essential is communion with Christ." [15]

28

But to confine our consideration of the Church in the New Testament to this one word is to miss the richness of the writers' understandings of the Christian community. We must try to leave the twentieth century—and our tendency to identify the Church with a building, an organization, a denomination, the ordained ministry, or some other specialized function —and think of it rather as a people called of God through Christ. It is through these images [16] or metaphors or figures of speech that we must feel our way into the New Testament way of denoting the Church.

People of God. One of the most illuminating of these images is that which we have already recognized as characteristic of the Old Testament, the people of God (*ho laos tou Theou*).[17] The image is either stated or implied more frequently than any other in the New Testament, and, as Minear has pointed out, "To apply this analogy to the Christian community was to assert an enduring solidarity with that Israel of whose story the Law and the Prophets provided the authoritative account." [18]

Luke 1:17 quotes from Mal. 4:5-6 and adds, "To make ready for the Lord a people prepared." Paul ordinarily uses the image through quotations from the Old Testament, as in II Cor. 6:16, in which he quotes a combination of several Old Testament passages, most directly from Ezek. 37:27, with clear application to the Christian community:

> I will live in them and move
> among them,
> and I will be their God,
> and they shall be my people.

In Rom. 9:25-26 he quotes rather freely from Hosea:

> Those who were not my people
> I will call "my people,"
> and her who was not my beloved

29

I will call "my beloved."
And in the very place where it was
    said to them, "You are not my
    people,"
they will be called "sons of the living God."

(See also Gal. 6:16, II Cor. 6:18, and so on.) Tit. 2:14 puts it in similar fashion, speaking of the work of Christ "who gave himself for us to redeem us from all iniquity and to purify for himself a people of his own who are zealous for good deeds." (See also Heb. 8:8-10.)

It is in I Peter that the metaphor stands out in its most unmistakable clarity. It does not matter greatly whether this be a letter, a sermon, or baptismal instruction, for the associations with the past give it a broad connotation.

Come to him, to that living stone, rejected by men but in God's sight chosen and precious; and like living stones be yourselves built into a spiritual house, to be a holy priesthood, to offer spiritual sacrifices acceptable to God through Jesus Christ. . . .

But you are a chosen race, a royal priesthood, a holy nation, God's own people, that you may declare the wonderful deeds of him who called you out of darkness into his marvelous light. Once you were no people but now you are God's people; once you had not received mercy but now you have received mercy.

—I Pet. 2:4-5, 9-10

It is this passage, of course, which has been most productive in the formation of the doctrine of the "priesthood of all believers," or of "the baptized," or of "the laity." Should this passage be ignored, however, the basis is present in the other New Testament images for a clear picture of the responsibility of the whole people before God. No statement makes clearer than this, however, that the people who are called of God through Jesus Christ are to "declare the wonderful deeds of him who called you out of darkness into his marvelous light."

Body of Christ. A second image which contributes to our

30

understanding of the Church is that of the body, used exclusively by Paul (and by the Pauline author of Ephesians if this book was not actually written by Paul himself). The most thorough discussion is found in I Cor. 12. The human body is described as both one and many: one body with many members, each having its distinctive and irreplaceable function in the totality. So the Church, Paul argues, is "one body in Christ," with members having different functions: apostles, prophets, teachers, workers of miracles, healers, helpers, administrators, speakers in various kinds of tongues. In spite of this diversity, however, Paul insists, "You are the body of Christ and individually members of it" (I Cor. 12:27). Christ is the head of the body, as he states more clearly in Col. 1:18.

Most of us probably find this image a bit difficult to take, for it may seem to indicate a kind of collectivism which we decry. Certainly it has led in Roman Catholicism and Eastern Orthodoxy to a view of the Church which makes the hierarchy the controller of the body. Perhaps the individualism which characterized the post-Reformation period was necessary to combat this kind of churchly imperialism. But two things must be noted: First, it is Christ who is the head, not his representative(s) on earth. And second, there are other images in the New Testament which must be set alongside this one for a complete understanding of the nature of the Church.[19]

Household of God. Thus we turn to a third set of images, those having to do with house, household, and family. This image is rooted in Jesus' statement concerning his followers: "Here are my mother and my brothers! For whoever does the will of my Father in heaven is my brother, and sister, and mother." (Matt. 12:49b-50; see also Mark 3:34-35; and Luke 8:19-21.) In Acts Christians are sometimes known simply as the "brethren" (Acts 15:22).

In Eph. 2:19 this evocative passage occurs: "So then you are no longer strangers and sojourners, but you are fellow citizens with the saints and members of the household of

God." In I Cor. 3:9 Paul addresses the Corinthians as "God's field, God's building." And in I Pet. 2:17 occurs this injunction: "Love the brotherhood." Then there is the long comparison of the Church with the family in Eph. 5:21–6:4; and though this most likely applies to the family first and to the Church second, its effect may be seen in both directions. In the family of God all divisions are broken down: "There is neither Jew nor Greek, there is neither slave nor free, there is neither male nor female; for you are all one in Christ Jesus." (Gal. 3:28; see also Rom. 10:12 and Col. 3:11.)

For many the family image is the most illuminating of all. For one who has known the close associations, the ties of love, the estrangement and reconciliation, the sin and forgiveness which characterize a good family, the Church may easily be seen as the larger "family of God." One is born into a family by biological birth through no act or choice of his own, as he is born into the Church by baptism. He must be cared for as an infant and child by the family, just as the Church, as a helper to the family, must nurture its children. Eventually a member of a human family must begin to assume for himself certain responsibilities, and finally he is put on his own but with his family as a continued source of aid. So the child must begin to assume responsibility for himself as he is able, and eventually he must become a fully covenanting member of the Church, accepting responsibility for his own acts. A child may become a prodigal son of his human family, just as he may also become a prodigal son of the Church. Yet he still "belongs" to his family, just as he still "belongs" to the Church. The family develops its unity as individual members interact with one another in estrangement and reconciliation, in sin and forgiveness, just as members of the Church, under Christ, must work out the manner in which their unity in Christ is implemented.[20] Like all analogies this one breaks down if pushed too far, but it is an instructive one. Indeed,

32

the Christian family is the Church in microcosm just as the Church is the family in macrocosm.

The Covenant Community. There is a fourth image which is only implied in the New Testament (perhaps most clearly in the "people of God" images) but which seems necessary to complete our understanding of the Church; that is, the Church as the covenant community. We have said that the biblical faith is essentially a covenant faith and that God acts anew in Jesus Christ to establish a new relationship with man. His people are thus the people of the new covenant.

It seems especially important to me that such an image be held in tension with that of the Body of Christ, for, as we have noted, this one may easily lead to a collectivistic concept if not properly understood. Jeremiah, Ezekiel, and the New Testament are all clear that each person is ultimately responsible himself before God. He is not an isolated individual (Kierkegaard notwithstanding), for he is in community. Yet Kierkegaard was right when he insisted that ultimately each person must decide for himself whether he will or will not be a Christian. Birth into a state church (or one of our "established" churches in the United States) makes a child a member of the larger family of God, to be sure, but it does not make him a practicing Christian. Only he can decide this. It is well to remember that it was Paul who emphasized the personal relationship of justification and reconciliation, even though he called the Church the Body of Christ. We become faithful sons of the Church only as we personally enter into the covenant relationship established by God through Christ, accepting its obligations as well as its benefits.

"Koinonia." One further term which we have used previously deserves consideration even though it is not, strictly speaking, a description of the Church as such, but rather of the quality of its life. This is the Greek word *koinonia*, which means "participation with someone in something." [21] Paul's

33

statement, previously quoted, is the key to its meaning: "You are all one in Christ Jesus" (Gal. 3:28b). It is the quality of life which comes into being in the quiet searching of a group for the meaning of life, of a group joined together in a common project in the Spirit of Christ, of a total congregation as it faces the problems of human existence in the Spirit of its Lord and Master. It is thus no human invention, no result of the manipulation of people by the use of group techniques, no automatic reality for church people met together for worship, for eating, for business; it is essentially due to the coming of the Spirit of God into the midst of folk who corporately open their lives to him.

We shall have more to say about this in a later chapter when we discuss the small fellowship and study group, for though it cannot be manufactured by human beings, they can place themselves in a situation where the Spirit of Christ is more likely to become real.

Common Themes. Are there any common themes running through these and other images in the New Testament? There appears to me to be at least three.

First, the Church is a *corporate reality*, a group of people, a *body* or a *family*, a *whole* people. Paul's order in I Cor. 12:27 is significant: "Now you are the body of Christ and individually members of it." We are first a body, then individuals, he says. John Wesley is quoted as saying there is no such thing as "solitary religion." God has used my parents, my pastors, my church-school teachers, and many other people as means for his grace. Further, this community has not only a *spatial* but also a *lineal* dimension: God has used Paul, and Augustine, and Luther, and Calvin, and Cranmer, and Wesley, and countless unnamed faithful ones as means for his grace finally to reach me! We are surrounded by a "cloud of witnesses" (Heb. 12:1) in time and space; we are part of the "communion of saints"; we are debtors to the neighbor

34

through whom Christ becomes real to us today and to all those through whom he has worked his miracle of grace for nineteen centuries.

The Church is a historic community with a life of its own, stemming from the Incarnation, continuing in both faithfulness and unfaithfulness down to our own time. We are called into this body; through it we respond personally to its Lord.

A second common theme is that *God is the chief actor in the drama of redemption,* calling the Church into being and sustaining it through the Holy Spirit. The Church is people, as Claude Welch has so aptly insisted; but as he also quickly asserts, it is not just any people but God's own people.[22] The Church is essentially the community of people sustained by the Spirit. It not only has historic roots; it is also a living, dynamic, pulsating, life-giving community, the redemptive community in which man meets his Lord. It may fail miserably in a particular time and place in being this, but in doing so it forfeits its right to be known as Christ's church. The Church must never become so enamored with the past that it fails to change as it responds to needs of the present moment.

A third common theme is one which is particularly crucial for this book; namely, *it is the whole people of God who constitute the Church,* clergy and laity together. However one makes the distinction between clergy and laity—if he makes one at all—it seems clear that the fullness of the Church according to the New Testament is found only in its total membership. It is difficult to ascertain any radical separation within the total body when it is addressed as "a chosen race, a royal priesthood, a holy nation, God's own people" (I Pet. 2:9a). So crucial indeed is this question for the remainder of these pages that we must discuss it in more detail now and return to it in a later section where it determines the precise position which must be maintained on practical matters pertaining to the life and work of the Church.

What Is the Ministry of the Church?

It is impossible to discuss adequately the nature of the Church, as we have done in the previous section, without considering its mission. So inseparable are the two that some theologians hesitate to divide them at all. And when we begin to discuss mission, we are involved in ministry, which immediately presents to us the question of the ordained ministry, or priesthood. The question can be stated in terms of a sharp issue: Does the special, ordained ministry grow out of the general ministry of the whole people of God? Or does it in itself constitute the Church? Or, to put it in other terms, did Christ call a special ministry, the apostles, whose commission is found in Jesus' answer to Peter's confession of the messiahship of Jesus, "You are Peter [Petros], and on this rock [petra] I will build my church"? (Matt. 16:18). Or did he call men to discipleship, including the twelve, and at Pentecost commission the whole body to a common ministry?

The former position is clearly that of the Roman Catholic Church, as Father Congar clearly indicates in his scholarly work on the laity in the Roman tradition. The priests, especially the bishops, constitute the structure, or esse (being) of the Church; and where there are no duly ordained bishops the Church does not exist in its fullness. These bishops are the successors of the apostles, and the ministry of the Church fundamentally comes through them. In contrast with the being of the Church is its life, made up of the total membership, clergy and laity alike. Its life—that "through which she fulfills her mission"—presupposes the "cooperation of the faithful" [23] (that is, the laity). But the laity are clearly of a secondary order to the clergy.[24]

In Eastern Orthodoxy the rigid dichotomy which arose in the Roman Church in the Middle Ages between clergy and laity was never so completely developed. Rather the conception of a co-ministry of people and priests has been consistently maintained in all areas except government and teaching. As one modern writer has said:

The Eucharist is celebrated by *the whole people*, but only when its chief [that is, the priest] is at its head, for without him there is no people; in the same way, there is no head unless the people are present also. According to the expression of Theodore of Mopsuestia, the bishop is "the mouthpiece of the Church" for it is through him and in him that the ministry of the priesthood accomplished by God's people is manifested. . . .

Like teaching, government is a special ministry in the Church for which special gifts are indispensable. . . . Church-government and teaching are prerogatives of those who are specially called, and not of the whole of God's people. . . . The bishop governs God's people not in his own name (*ex sese*) and not as a "right" (as if he received the power from the people), but in the name of God, because he is set by God "in Christ" for the ministry of government.[25]

The laity, however, exercises "judgment" in matters of teaching and government, examining what happens through their gifts of investigation.[26] The fact remains, then, that there is a division between the two orders which, though not nearly so rigid as that of Roman Catholicism, is nevertheless real.

Protestantism, as we shall see in a later chapter, has had a divided mind on this subject. One contemporary scholar of the Church of Scotland argues, for example, in much the fashion of the Roman apologist for a doctrine of the Church which views it as constituted by the apostles and their successors, the set-apart clergy. "When we think of the Church as the Body of Christ," he writes, "we have to think of it in terms of the mission of the Son from the Father which through the Apostolic Foundation is inserted into history reaching out through the ages to the parousia." [27] Thus the ordained ministry of the Church is not from the whole Church upward but from Christ downward to the whole Church. The ministry does not represent the Church before God, but rather Christ to the Church.[28] This means, he concludes, "that the ministry of the Church is not to be thought of as a function of the people or of their delegates. The ministry of the Church is not democratically grounded and built up from the members of the Church so as to represent them before God." [29]

Torrance's terms "democratically grounded" and "built up from the members of the Church so as to represent them before God" seem to me to cloud the issue and to offer a false alternative. By this he seems to indicate that (a) either we must have a special ministry which derives its authority by the historic succession directly from Christ, or (b) we must have a special ministry which derives its authority from the congregation and—somewhat inconsistently—represents the laity before God. If I read the New Testament aright, there is a third possibility; namely, that the entire Church derives its ministry from Christ, and the set-apart ministry, because of this common ministry, exercises certain functions in the name of Christ on behalf of the whole congregation.

In other words, the ministry of word and sacrament was entrusted to the whole Church, which in turn developed a special ministry beginning in New Testament times for the fulfillment of certain aspects of this total ministry. The representative character of the special ministry does not necessarily mean that those who exercise it are democratically chosen (though in some communions this is essentially what happens), nor certainly that they perform their ministry in terms of the whims of the people. The Church is not, as it tended to become in nineteenth-century America, a democratic institution; rather it is a theocracy, with Christ as its head. There are some things a congregation may vote on, but there are others on which it ought not. But whether it votes or does not vote, it, as a totality, is responsible to God just as the special ministry is. And the responsibility of the whole people includes, as the Eastern Orthodox would say, judging whether or not the special ministry is faithfully performing its functions.

If this point seems to have been labored with undue technicalities, it is due to the fact that there appears to be no other way to present it. For that matter there are many issues which have not been considered at all, questions which would lead us into even more difficult problems. It does seem to me important, however, that we assert the general New Testament witness, in spite of problems like the special place which Paul assigns to the apostles, to a total ministry of the entire people of God, with special ministries set aside within the general body. In other words, we ought to begin with the total Church and from there proceed to consider the set-apart ministry, rather than in the way in which both Congar and Torrance begin.

This means that the Church can never be understood in its fullness as being constituted by the clergy, with the laity as second-class members. Clerical ordination must be understood against the background of the general ordination of all Christians through baptism. The laity are not a secondary order; they are, in fact, the first order, for basically all are *laos*, and those set aside for special leadership functions are first lay, then clerical.

Indeed, some contemporary theologians prefer to say that the Church *is* mission or ministry, rather than that it *has* a mission or ministry. This manner of putting the case suggests that each member is a part of the ministry, even though some are set apart for special ministries. It follows also that this ministry is to be exercised not only within the organized church but also in the world. The Christian's vocation is to serve God in all realms of life: Church, occupation, family, politics, social life, and all the rest. Of this we shall have much more to say later.

39

Before proceeding further with this discussion, however, let us turn to a brief summary of historical data in order to see how the Church has dealt with the question of the laity during its nineteen centuries of history.

NOTES

1. Cf. Reuel Howe, *Man's Need and God's Action* (Greenwich, Conn.: The Seabury Press, 1953). Paul Tillich's "method of correlation" is implied here. See his *Systematic Theology* (Chicago: The University of Chicago Press, 1951), I, especially 59-66.
2. Victor Paul Furnish, "Let's Avoid Cheap Biblical Unity," *Christian Advocate*, V (Mar. 30, 1961), p. 6.
3. The ideas contained in this section are dependent upon a number of contemporary sources, and the following books are only representative of those available. For an elementary introduction to these ideas, see Bernhard W. Anderson, *The Unfolding Drama of the Bible* (Reflection Book; rev. ed.; New York: Association Press, 1957). A somewhat more advanced presentation of the same point of view is found in his book, *Rediscovering the Bible* (Haddam House; New York: Association Press, 1951). C. H. Dodd's *The Bible Today* (New York: The Macmillan Company, 1946) is also helpful. An unusually clear and perceptive treatment of the covenant theme is found in Suzanne de Dietrich's *The Witnessing Community: The Biblical Record of God's Purpose* (Philadelphia: The Westminster Press, 1958). A somewhat more technical treatment is found in B. Davie Napier's *From Faith to Faith: Essays on Old Testament Literature* (New York: Harper & Brothers, 1955), especially the Introduction and Chap. 2.
4. It does not seem to me relevant for our discussion that most biblical scholars would insist that these two stories come from different sources and were only later brought together. In understanding the message of the Bible, we must recognize that at times the total message is more important than particular matters of historical criticism.
5. Again it does not seem to me relevant for our purposes to determine whether we are dealing with history. The significant thing, even when it is accepted as history, is the meaning behind the story.
6. Anderson, *The Unfolding Drama*, p. 39.
7. From *The Witnessing Community* by Suzanne de Dietrich. Copyright 1958, W. L. Jenkins. The Westminster Press. By permission.
8. This is a phrase used by Anderson in *The Unfolding Drama*, Study III.
9. *Ibid.*, pp. 62-63.
10. De Dietrich, *op. cit.*, p. 129.
11. *Ibid.*, pp. 129-30.
12. *Ibid.*, pp. 131-34.
13. J. S. Whale, *Victor and Victim: The Christian Doctrine of Redemption* (New York: Cambridge University Press, 1960), especially Chaps. 1-4.
14. I have developed my understanding of the Church in more detail in

The Church Redemptive (Nashville: Abingdon Press, 1958), Chaps. 2-5.

15. Karl Ludwig Schmidt, The Church, Part II of Bible Key Words, from Gerhard Kittel's Theologisches Wörterbuch zum Neuen Testament, trans. and ed. J. R. Coates (New York: Harper & Brothers, 1951), pp. 8, 21.

16. I am much indebted to Paul S. Minear for this way of thinking of the Church in the New Testament. I first was influenced in this direction in a seminar in New Testament Theology which he conducted at Yale Divinity School during the academic year 1957-58 and in which he provided us with mimeographed material as yet unpublished. He has recently had published what is undoubtedly the finest book in its field, Images of the Church in the New Testament (Philadelphia: The Westminster Press, 1960). In this book he discusses ninety-six images.

17. Besides many of the books indicated in note 2, see also H. J. Kraus, The People of God in the Old Testament ("World Christian Books No. 22" [New York: Association Press, 1958]).

18. Minear, op. cit., p. 70.

19. There are three ways of thinking of the "Body of Christ" as a term used for the Church: (a) as a literal description of the Church in terms of an extension of the Incarnation (as in E. L. Mascall, Christ, the Christian and the Church [New York: Longmans, Green & Co., 1946], especially pp. 112, 161); (b) as only one of the "images" or metaphors in the New Testament designating the corporate life of the faithful (Minear, op. cit., Chap. 7; Claude Welch, The Reality of the Church [New York: Charles Scribner's Sons, 1958], Chap. 5); and (c) as a "root metaphor," that is, possessing more authority than the others. (Geddes MacGregor, Corpus Christi: The Nature of the Church According to the Reformed Tradition [Philadelphia: The Westminster Press, 1959], Chap. 9, especially pp. 167-69). Arguments for (a) and (c) seem to me something less than convincing, though it may be argued that no other metaphor is quite as adequate as this one.

20. Cf. F. D. Dillistone, The Structure of the Divine Society (Philadelphia: The Westminster Press, 1951), pp. 221-22.

21. I have discussed this word more thoroughly in The Church Redemptive, op. cit., pp. 50-53.

22. Welch, op. cit., pp. 60-81.

23. Congar, op. cit., p. 249.

24. Ibid., p. xxvii.

25. N. Afanassieff, "The Ministry of the Laity in the Church," in A Symposium on the Laity (published by the Department of the Laity, World Council of Churches, 1958; reprinted from The Ecumenical Review, X [Apr., 1958]), pp. 33, 34, 35. Used by permission of the World Council of Churches.

26. Afanassieff, pp. 34, 35.

27. T. F. Torrance, Royal Priesthood; Scottish Journal of Theology Occasional Papers, No. 3 (Edinburgh and London: Oliver and Boyd, Ltd., 1955), p. 28.

28. Ibid., especially pp. 39-40.

29. Ibid., p. 40.

CHAPTER 3

HISTORICAL BACKGROUND

It is within neither the scope nor the purpose of this book to present a systematic and detailed account of the laity in its historical development. Historical perspective is of sufficient importance in our attempt to understand the present role of the laity in the Church, however, that a brief historical summary seems appropriate. This history is viewed in the following major steps: no essential difference in the orders of the ministry in the New Testament; the gradual separation in the early church of clergy and laity, with the laity still holding considerable status; the crystalization of the trend toward separation in the early Middle Ages; protests against it in monasticism and in the heretical and sectarian movements; the breaking of the rigid wall between clergy and laity at the time of the Reformation; the fulfillment of this break in the radical Reformation; the coming to fruition of this trend in American Christianity; the increasing tendency in twentieth-century American Christianity toward professionalism; and the reassertion of the ministry of the laity in the contemporary ecumenical movement. For our purposes the three most important periods are the New Testament, the Reformation, and the modern American; hence major emphasis will be placed on these three.

The Early Church

As we have already seen, the earliest picture we receive of the Church in the New Testament, especially in the letters of Paul, is one in which there were "diversities of gifts" but "one body and one Spirit" (Rom. 12:4-8; I Cor. 12:12-31a, Eph. 4: 4-16). To be sure, the story in Acts 6 indicates the appointment of deacons, or servers (Acts 6:1-6), at an early period in the Church. It is worthy of note, however, that one of the seven, Stephen, soon met his martyrdom not because of the exercise of his ministry as a deacon but rather because of his preaching (Acts 7:2–8:1).

It is significant that Paul always lists the apostles first in his lists of gifts or ministries. There seems no reason to question the conclusion that the apostles (at first the twelve) possessed an unusual authority, derived partly from their proximity to the earthly ministry of Jesus.[1] It was, for example, the twelve who laid their hands on the deacons (Acts 6:6). Clement, in the late first century, even asserts that the apostles had provided for others who would succeed them.[2] Many have argued that references such as these provide a basis for "apostolic succession"; that is, an unbroken line of special ministers going back through the bishops to the original apostles. Anthony Hanson has recently argued cogently that Clement did not have any such thing in mind; he was concerned with "a continuation of function, but not of a continuation of an order, bishop ordaining bishop and so on."[3]

The issue is far too complicated for us to discuss it here, though its significance in ecumenical discussions cannot be denied. Three comments may be made in passing, however. Even if it can be proved that the succession of bishops can be traced back to the apostles, there seems to be undue emphasis placed upon a kind of mechanical process of succession in many discussions of the issue. On the other hand, those who deny the reality of succession altogether tend to underesti-

43

mate the significance of historic continuity in the Church. Yet the authority of the bishop or the clergyman ought not to be derived from his relationship to a representative of Christ, even an apostle, but from Christ himself through the office of the Holy Spirit.

In any case, by the time of the Pastoral epistles (I and II Timothy and Titus), probably rather late in the first century in their present form, bishops (*episkopoi* or overseers), and deacons (*diakonoi*, or servants, attendants, ministers) had developed as church officials (I Tim. 3:1-13). Whether or not the elders (*presbuteroi*) mentioned in I Tim. 5:17 (and in Acts 11:30; 14:23; 15:2, 4, 6, 22, 23; 16:4; and 21:18) represent the same office as the bishop we shall not attempt to settle here, for it has been and continues to be a point of controversy among theologians and church historians.[4] To say the least, there is no evidence that the *episkopoi* were anything more than overseers of local congregations, a situation which prevailed for some years to come. Indeed, the picture one gets from the New Testament is of a fluid and flexible ministry, with some tendency toward more fixed forms near the end of the period.

This growing distinctiveness finds further expression in Clement, who differentiates between the responsibilities of four orders in the conduct of the liturgy, or worship: the "high priest" (bishops?), the priests (elders?), the levites (deacons?), and the laity. "The layman," he writes, "is bound by the layman's code." [5] A short time later, probably in the first or second decade of the second century, Ignatius went so far as to say that you cannot have a church without bishops (overseers of local congregations), presbyters (officers of a local congregation), and deacons.[6] He further states that the bishop, or someone whom he authorizes, must celebrate the Eucharist, and further that he must authorize baptisms and love-feasts.[7] It should be noted that one of the reasons, if not the main one, for this setting up of authoritative officers was

Ignatius' concern that the Church not be corrupted by heresy. Such heresies as Gnosticism and Docetism, as reflected in the Johannine literature, were already of some consequence; and with the lack of learning of most Christians the leaders of the congregations (bishops) had as one of their chief functions the preservation of pure doctrine, as well as the keeping of the Church from schism.[8]

By the time of Irenaeus in the late second century the stratification had become clearer, so that he writes: "Therefore it is right to obey the presbyters in the Church, those, that is, who possess the succession from the apostles, as I have shown, who, together with their succession in the episcopate, received the sure gift of truth according to the good pleasure of the Father." [9] Even so, Irenaeus seems to have had no intention of establishing a completely sacerdotal view of the ministry, for in another place of the same work he asserts, "I have shown that all the disciples of the Lord are Levites and priests." [10] Shortly thereafter, in the early third century, Cyprian further widened the division between clergy and laity when he clearly set forth the divine institution of the episcopacy.[11]

By the mid-third century the bishops had assumed supervisory power over the lesser clergy, and the clergy had assumed more control over the laity. To be sure, there could still be a lay teacher such as Origen was during the early part of his life —though it is significant that he was removed from his position three times by Bishop Demetrius, largely because of alleged insubordination, and he finally accepted ordination, perhaps to make his status more secure. George Williams' statement about Origen indicates what was happening, or perhaps had already happened, in the Church: "Origen was, in a sense, the last of the Christian charismatic and independent teachers." [12] Perhaps Seeberg is also correct when he concludes that with Callistus, the Bishop of Rome in the early third century who assumed the right to declare the forgiveness of sins, the idea of the Church as the holy people of God came to an end—at least in Rome.[13] In other places the process was slower in development and never went so far in the East as it did in the West.

The Medieval Church

By the time Christianity was established as the official religion of the Roman Empire, the process of separation of clergy and laity was fairly clearly established. In the Constitution of the Holy Apostles, probably from the early fourth century, the lay person is exhorted to honor the bishop "as to a good shepherd," to "love him, reverence him as his lord, as his master, as the high priest of God, as a teacher of piety." The bishop is described as "the keeper of knowledge, the mediator between God and you in the several parts of your divine worship." [14]

As the Middle Ages wore on, the division between clergy and laity increased so that in the West the priest stood at Communion, the layman knelt. The priest partook of both elements, the laity, only of one.[15] With the imposition of celibacy in the eleventh century—though it was not yet universally obeyed—the demarcation had reached its final stage,[16] a situation which still prevails in Roman Catholicism. As we have noted, the Eastern Church never developed quite the rigid division betwen the two orders as occurred in the West, with the laity still possessing the prerogative to exercise the ministry of "judgment" and "investigation" with respect to teaching and governing.[17] Yet practice has placed relatively little emphasis on the responsibility of the laity in taking the initiative in such matters.

There were, of course, exceptions to this general rule. For example, the Christian ruler was expected to act as an agent of the Church in his position of responsibility. Charlemagne is the prime example of the ruler who took his Christian responsibility in great seriousness, though there were others, both before and after Charlemagne, who made substantial contributions to the partial Christianizing of the social order and the amelioration of the harsh conditions of life which had characterized the Roman world. In general, however, it may be concluded that the Church, through the hierarchy, exercised fairly complete control over the religious life of the laity and to a great extent over the entire culture.

There are reasons for this development apart from the human weakness of the clergy which made them enjoy the increased prestige the higher status of their calling created. For example, as the number of converts increased, and especially with the great influx of members after Constantine recognized Christianity, both the fervor and the intellectual level of the laity markedly decreased. As we have seen, the reason first given for the increased power of the bishop was that he might guarantee the preservation of right doctrine. The condition prevailed throughout the Middle Ages with little effort being made to change the situation. Periodic efforts were made, to be sure—for example, those by Charlemagne—to provide more adequate education; and it may be that the literacy of the laity was at a higher level than we have generally been led to believe. But generally speaking most laymen were unable to assume any position of responsibility.

We must also bear in mind that the structure of feudalistic society was such that there was no disposition either by clergy or by ruling princes to allow the laity the kind of independence which could have led to responsible churchmanship. It was not until the development of some degree of individual initiative, either in the economic or political realm or in both, that people saw themselves as anything other than subjects of the ruling powers. Even if one argues that the impetus for changes in the social realm came partly from changes in theological thinking, the condition prevailing among the common people is not measurably affected. Leadership, whatever its source, was necessary before any sizable group of people could begin to see themselves as responsible personally for either Church

47

or world. Whatever the precise relationship between Protestantism and democracy may be, both required and encouraged a sense of personal responsibility which made necessary a rethinking of the relationship between clergy and laity.

Monasticism and the Sects

Although the organized church gave little place for lay activity during this long period, not all laymen were content with the situation. Indeed, as the opportunities for lay participation in the life of the Church decreased and as the Church increasingly compromised with the world, Christian asceticism and eventually monasticism arose. Many of the early ascetic movements such as Montanism (late second, third centuries) were declared heretical, but not all. Individual asceticism stems from the early period also, and the ascetic was more likely to be a layman than a priest. This kind of personal asceticism was still enjoined by Jerome in about 400, in a letter to Laeta concerning the rearing of her daughter,[18] and in a somewhat later one to Gaudentius, also pertaining to the education of a daughter.

In the fourth century the formation of communities of ascetics, at first of men but later women, became more and more common. Most of these participants were originally laymen or women, though the trend in most lay monastic groups for men has always been toward ordination as a more common practice, and this was true in the early period. So much of the original initiative and energy were lay, however, that it may be said to be originally a lay movement.

Further, throughout the history of monasticism to the present day laymen have played a significant role. Although Francis of Assisi was a deacon, he considered his order essentially a lay order. Women's orders have, of course, always been lay in character. In our own day the Reformed Community of Taizé in southern France has a majority of laymen. It may

48

be argued that once a lay person withdraws from ordinary life he ceases to be a layman in the real sense. Father Congar, for example, considers the lay or ordained monk in a class different from the lay or ordained man of the world.[19] Most of the orders, however, have sent their members into the world to perform all manner of services: agriculture, teaching, nursing, social work, and the like. The lay impetus cannot be ignored.

Not all the movements which began within the Church were tolerated by the Church, nor should they have been. Gnosticism, for example, was one of the earliest major movements which was rejected. It is interesting to note, however, that some of these heresies placed a greater emphasis on the laity. Even Gnosticism, with its insistence that each person must attain *gnosis* (secret knowledge), is to some extent of this order. Later, Montanism was based partly on a greater emphasis on the laity, a condition illustrated by Tertullian's insistence after he became a Montanist that "where three are, there is the Church, albeit they be laics." [20]

By and large in the early Middle Ages monasticism seems to have absorbed those who both in earlier and in later times might have become schismatics. But as the Church assumed even more control over life in the later Middle Ages, an increasing restlessness characterized many people. Lay uprisings against the clergy were not uncommon,[21] and out of these grew a semi-Christian group known as the Cathari. For our purposes the most interesting aspect of the sect, heretical though it was, was its emphasis on lay Christianity, lay preaching, and the lay apostolate.[22] The groups spread throughout much of south central Europe in the twelfth and thirteenth centuries.

During the same period an orthodox movement arose, at first in France, later in northern Italy, under the leadership of a merchant of Lyons named Peter Waldo. Desiring at first only to do missionary work within the Church, the group was later ousted and formed themselves into a separate group with

49

considerable lay emphasis.[23] The group, the Waldensians, still exists, primarily in northern Italy. When Francis of Assisi came along not long afterward, the Church had learned its lesson and managed to keep his energies channeled within the structure of the Church.

In these and other ways protests were already being made against the organized Church more than a century before Wycliffe and Huss.

The Reformation

Just as the character of the Church in the Middle Ages cannot be understood apart from the culture of those centuries, so the Church of the Reformation must be seen in relation to movements within society of its time. These forces have a direct relationship to the increase of lay emphasis within the Church.

The establishment of the universities and the gradual growth of learning from the eleventh century onward; the growth of humanism and out of that the Renaissance, or revival of the arts and humane learning; the increasing development of world trade and eventually the coming of early capitalism; and the rise of the nation-state, with at least incipient democratic tendencies—all are a part of the picture in the period preceding and accompanying the Reformation. The date of the Magna Charta, a milestone in the development of English democracy, is 1215, more than two and one-half centuries before the birth of Luther. The great Dante died a century after the Magna Charta, and the discovery of the New World occurred when Luther was nine years old. The times were ripe for new forms of church life when Luther nailed his theses to the church door at Wittenberg; and though the Reformation cannot be understood merely as a social movement, neither can it be understood apart from the social situation.

We have already noted in the twelfth and thirteenth centuries the emergence of reform movements, both within and without the Roman Church, both orthodox and heretical. In the fourteenth and fifteenth centuries came Wycliffe in England and Huss in Bohemia. Wycliffe's chief passion was to make it possible for the laity to read the Bible as the basis for independent study and criticism of the Church. The influence of his work in translating the Scriptures, along with that of William Tyndale, Miles Coverdale, and John Rogers, was considerable. Out of the Hussite movement grew the forerunner of the Moravian Brethren, led by a layman, Peter von Chelzic, whose goal was to form a brotherhood in which all persons might live a completely consecrated life.[24] These and other movements paved the way for the major Reformation stemming from Luther in the sixteenth century.

It is not within the scope of this book to describe in detail the work of the reformers or the Reformation itself.[25] Suffice it to say that whatever else it did—and it obviously did much more—it broke down the rigid wall between clergy and laity, and an attempt was made to assert once more the idea of the Church as the whole people. Luther's insistence upon the common priesthood of all Christians is crucial at this point. He did not mean, as is often believed, only that each person has a direct relationship with God without the mediation of a priest, but also that each person is mutually responsible for his neighbor. "We are all priests," wrote Luther, "insofar as we are Christians, but those whom we call priests are ministers selected from our midst to act in our name, and their priesthood is our ministry." [26] Luther could not have made such a statement had he not held firmly to the idea that the whole Church is called by Christ into ministry, that all men are directly responsible to him, and that they are thus mutually responsible for one another.

The practical difficulties which Luther encountered in carrying out this principle were so great that it was never completely implemented. Kraemer suggests several reasons for this situation. One hindrance was the fact that the idea of the established church was not denied by the main-line reformers, and this tended toward a conservatism inimical to the New Testament pattern. Further, the force of habit made the laity often reluctant to change to a more responsible position. Likewise, the Reformation emphasis on preaching tended to set up the preacher as the one who knew the faith and who was to inform the ignorant laity. The preacher tended to become the specialized "theologian" who was above the unlearned laity. Finally, the dependence of the reformers upon the princes and political magistrates for carrying through many of the reforms tended to perpetuate a hierarchical structure.[27] When one considers the tremendous amount of education needed in order to create an informed laity, he can appreciate more fully the tendency toward a more conservative approach to the laity in the later Luther.

Although none of the other reformers ever quite enunciated the idea of the priesthood of the laity with Luther's clarity, it was in the background of much that they did. Indeed, in many ways the practical implications of the idea were implemented more fully in the Calvinistic, or Reformed, churches than in the Lutheran, with the elders given enough control that they were able on occasion to influence what Calvin himself did.[28] It was, as Franklin Littell has indicated, the inclusion of "discipline" as the third "mark" of the Church which provided a structure for lay activity unlike that of Lutheranism. It was not alone preaching and the sacraments which constituted the Church, as in the Lutheran and Anglican traditions, but also the disciplined, or ordered, life.[29] Unlike the other two marks, which pertain to the clergy more directly, this one involves the laity in a specific fashion.

Puritanism, as it developed first in England and later in New England, went even further in its emphasis on the laity, and some of its offshoots were dissatisfied even with Puritanism. Nor should the significant gains for the laity in the main-line groups be minimized: in such areas as participation in worship, the translation of the Bible into the vernacular, the emphasis on the Christian family, the growth of education for the masses, and the emphasis on the Christian's exercising his calling in the secular world, great gains were made.

The "Radical" Groups

There were those who believed that the main-line reformers had not gone far enough, however. They insisted upon a more radical change, with the word "radical" used in its original sense as pertaining to the changing of the fundamental form of something—in this instance with respect to a return to the New Testament form of the Church. The leaders of this movement believed that reform of the present church was inadequate; what was needed was the restoration of the primitive Church. It was in this so-called "left wing" of the Reformation that the laity, not only in theory but also in practice, achieved a status unlike that which they had had since New Testament times. Until recently church historians have often dealt unsympathetically with these groups, tending to look at them through the eyes of their contemporary enemies in the main-line churches of the Reformation. Recent writing has thrown new light on the groups, however, and their contributions to the continuing reformation of the Church are now being reassessed.[30]

Most of these groups insisted upon both a new understanding of the laity, much like Luther's emphasis on the priesthood of all Christians, and the implementation of the idea in church life. The laity were not a lesser order than the clergy, in any sense servile to the clergy, but rather as much responsible for the faith as they were in the primitive church. They were, to use Littell's phrase, again to become "carriers of the faith." Thus in many of these groups there were not, strictly speaking, clergy and laity, but only believers, all of whom were to assume

53

full responsibility for the Christian community even though they appointed officers who exercised special functions.[31]

Whether or not this radical view is functionally possible is not our present task to determine, though it is interesting to note that only one of these groups has remained almost completely nonclerical; namely, the Society of Friends, or Quakers. Stemming from the work of George Fox in the second half of the seventeenth century, this group still usually only "records" ministers as a recognition of their special gift of ministry, with no clergy as such.[32]

With a few exceptions these groups never gained much of a foothold in Europe. Although the main-line Reformation churches continued in many ways to emphasize the laity,[33] the tendency toward a new clericalism soon asserted itself among the state churches. Perhaps the Church of Scotland is as notable an exception to this as is found in Europe, but even here the Iona Community, a twentieth-century "reform" movement in that group, has had as one of its aims an emphasis on the ministry of the laity. By and large European Christianity has become clerically centered, so that Kraemer is probably right when he asserts that "the laity in the Churches regards itself as of minor and subsidiary significance." [34] One of the significant changes which have occurred since World War II in European Protestantism is a rediscovery of the importance of the laity.[35]

The situation has been considerably different in North America, however, and will be discussed in more detail.

The Laity in the New World [36]

No attempt will be made here to pretend that the American colonies were from their founding paragons of democratic virtues, or that the churches suddenly entered upon a period of New Testament fervor and vigor. Such is simply not the case. The motives which sent the colonists to the new world were varied, and even those who came for purposes of religious freedom, such as the Puritans in New England, were unwilling to extend the freedom they desired to dissident groups. It was, indeed, never the intention of the Puritans, even in their own churches, that the whole people should rule but only that they be ruled by the "specially elect of God," [37] which included laymen. This meant that some of the laity assumed both greater interest in and responsibility for the life of the Church than was the case of the major groups in Europe.

In Puritan New England, then, the church elders exercised great control of the churches, laymen often performing clerical duties when no clergyman was present. Necessity, in fact, played a significant role in the assumption of much lay responsibility not only in the seventeenth century but also in the following two, and it affected Anglicanism as well as Congregationalism and the groups which developed later. For even the Anglican churches in the South were changed in the American environment, partly because of necessity and partly because of the spirit of independence which gradually developed—so much so, in fact, that the Archbishop of Canterbury is reported, in 1697, as expressing surprise that clergymen might "be removed like domestic Servants by a Vote of the Vestry." [38]

Soon the lay emphasis was given greater impetus by the establishing of groups which had been influenced by the more radical side of the Reformation. The earliest, the Baptists, are associated with Roger Williams and the establishing of Rhode Island as an asylum of religious freedom in the mid-seventeenth century. Soon the Quakers began migrating to the New World, at first to Rhode Island and later to the colony chartered by William Penn in 1681. The democratic tendencies in political and social life also began to flower in the eighteenth century, leading to the War for Independence in 1776. These forces provided a receptive environment for the growth of church groups emphasizing lay control.

Without denying the theological basis for the greater emphasis on the laity, it cannot be understood apart from sociocultural forces at work in the emerging nation. Two factors are of special importance. One is the frontier, which exercised a continuing influence on American institutions up to at least the present century. Not only did the free atmosphere of the frontier affect the churches as well as other institutions; there was also the necessity for great individual initiative on the part of church members. Had laymen not taken an active part in the life of the Church, it could hardly have existed at all, since the visits of clergymen were infrequent.

The second factor in this development is the principle, established by the Bill of Rights, of the separation of church and state which put the churches on their own without either state support or control. The voluntaryistic principle was already present in the covenant emphasis found especially in Congregationalism and Presbyterianism. Without state support, all the churches became dependent upon voluntary financial support and the principle was encouraged in other areas also.[39] As an early nineteenth-century writer put it for his European readers: "Thus have Americans been trained to exercise the same energy, self-reliance, and enterprise in the cause of religion which they exhibit in other affairs." [40]

To call attention to these environmental factors is not to deny the importance of internal factors in the development of the churches. It is difficult to determine, however, how adequately grounded theologically the concern for laymen was, though the practice, as we have seen, was common from the beginning. As more and more of the groups from the radical Reformation migrated to America, the incipient tendencies were encouraged, since these groups were by their nature lay-centered. The Mennonites, for example, had arrived in the late seventeenth and early eighteenth centuries; and somewhat later groups such as the Dunkers, the Ephrata Society, and the Moravians had begun to seek refuge in the New World.[41] Further, the first Great Awakening, the religious revival which swept the colonies in the mid-eighteenth century, had far-reaching results in the awakening of lay fervor and the setting of informal patterns of church life which increased the influence of the laity.[42]

Five conditions, then, converged to bring the laity to a position of eminence in American Protestantism in the nineteenth century: the incipient tendencies toward lay control and initiative from the beginning of the colonies; the democratic milieu of political and social life, especially on the frontier; the migration to the New World of the more radical "free" churches; the effects of the Great Awakening; and the growth in the nineteenth century of churches which confirmed the trend. The fruition of the movement can be seen most clearly in church government.

We have seen how Congregationalism in New England was from the beginning controlled by selected laymen (the elders). Somewhat later the Baptists began to emerge, and in the nineteenth century their growth was rapid. The less-known groups, some of which have been mentioned, also increased in the eighteenth century. Further, an indigenous group, the Disciples of Christ, arose in the early nineteenth century partly because Alexander Campbell felt that other churches, including the Baptist, did not go far enough. So completely lay-centered did he consider the Church that he regarded the minister "as simply a special worker chosen by a congregation to have oversight of one voluntary society, who, when he leaves that society, has no office in any other in consequence of his being an officer in that." [43]

It is not solely in congregationally controlled churches that the influence of laymen can be seen, however. Presbyterian churches were, as late as the early nineteenth century, sometimes confused with the Congregational even though they were governed by representative laymen rather than by the entire congregation. The Episcopal Church from its organization in 1789 contained provisions for lay representation in the General Convention,[44] and the vestry, composed of laymen, is the ruling body of the local parish.[45] Methodism, which in some ways placed a great deal of emphasis on the laity, resisted the admission of laymen into its official bodies; and it was only after a long and sometimes bitter struggle that they were seated in the General Conferences of the two major Methodist churches in the 1870's.[46] It is significant that laymen were not satisfied with a clerically controlled denomination, as many clergymen also were not, and the long struggle was the result.

It was not only in church government that laymen assumed a larger share in the life of American Protestantism during the nineteenth century; they were also responsible for, and played a large role in, several movements which emerged in the organized church. The earliest and best known is the Sunday school, which from its beginning in late eighteenth-century England was a lay movement. It remained that during the following century, and still is to a considerable extent in spite of the professionalism which has developed within recent decades. Laymen also played a significant role in the youth movements which grew up both outside the organized church (the Young Men's and Young Women's Christian Association) and inside (the interdenominational Christian Endeavor and the comparable denominational groups). It was the women of the church, often with the disapproval of the clergy, who brought to fruition the various women's groups several decades before women were granted equal rights within the denominations. (In some they still do not have such rights.) In these and other ways laymen in the nineteenth century insisted upon a larger share in the interior life of the churches.

Laymen also exercised leadership and influence in the social movements of the century. This was especially true of the antislavery movement and, later, of the temperance movement. In spite of well-known examples to the contrary, there are also many instances of businessmen who attempted to exercise their Christian vocation in business. Nor can the many examples of philanthropy to church, social, and educational causes be ignored as being in many instances expressions of Christian lay concern. Not all the social reforms which have occurred in American life during the past century can be attributed to Christian laymen, though neither is it possible to deny the Christian impulse as an important factor in the total picture.

The picture one receives from surveying nineteenth-century American Protestantism, then, is one which involves much lay interest, participation, and concern.

Twentieth-Century Problems and Prospects

Most of the movements which originated in the nineteenth century have been continued in the twentieth. In fact, the various "activities" of local congregations are often so great as to demand the services of many laymen for their implementation. Further, the "sect" groups which have developed within recent decades are often quite lay-centered. Such "free churches," to use the European term to describe them, have, by and large, had little concern for ordination and hence the line of demarcation between clergy and laity tends to be obscured. In many, few if any requirements are made the basis for ordination, and in some of the fringe groups a process close to self-ordination exists.

The standard American churches, on the other hand, have assumed many of the characteristics of established churches, becoming to a great extent cultural institutions, as was indicated in an earlier chapter. Henry Steele Commager, in appraising the changing role of the church in American culture, concludes that they now tend to serve as social organizations.[47]

59

The development of the "program-centered church," in which a large variety of activities is carried on, many of which are only peripherally associated with the major purpose of the Church, has necessitated the use of many laymen. But this is the point at which a serious question must be raised: are laymen really being the people of God, or are they being used, often by professional staff personnel, to direct recreation, lead clubs, chair committees, raise money, get members, and otherwise carry out a program which is often only a reflection of the best aspects of society?

The expansion of the programs of local congregations has been accompanied by a parallel growth of national boards and agencies set up to plan and promote particular aspects of the program. While such agencies are normally set up to serve a genuine need, the temptation for such groups is to conceive of their work as being promotional rather than advisory. As a consequence many local church people feel that they are so busy carrying out plans from higher headquarters that there is hardly time for them to be the Church in their local community. Further, there seems to be no essential difference in this respect between most churches with a congregational polity and those with a connectional structure.[48] To raise questions about the present character of such agencies is not to suggest that they can or ought to be abolished. There does seem to be a need for rethinking the nature of the Church on all levels and, in connection with this, the relationship between the various levels of church organization.

Another result of the expansion of programs is the development of the multiple staff for larger congregations. This is probably an inevitable concomitant to the growth of specialization within the general culture. Here too the temptation is for such persons to think of themselves as "directing the army of lay workers," a concept which unfortunately was incorporated into the most common title given to specialists in Christian education, the director of Christian education. Some progress has been made in the developing of the idea of the "team ministry" in place of the "multiple staff," but how deeply this concept has influenced current practice is difficult to judge. To a great extent it would appear that employed church personnel, whether lay or ordained, often think of themselves as professional leaders rather than ministers with a specialized function. Since many such people are laymen, Hendrik Kraemer has coined the term "the clericalized laity" to denote them.[49]

This growing professionalism has affected the American churches' understanding of the laity and has led to a danger equivalent to the clericalism of the European churches. Status, influence, and office are often defined by professional position rather than by clerical ordination, both on the local church level and on the national board level. It is easy, then, for the professional man to use laymen to help him get the job done in much the same way that a professional group worker in a social agency uses lay people as group leaders. Even the meaning of "lay" is often interpreted as applying to the untrained, nonprofessional worker in contrast with the trained, professional worker, even though this was not, as we have indicated, the original meaning of the word. Although clericalism has never been a real problem for American Protestantism, it has within recent decades fallen into what may be as insidious a disease; that is, professionalism.

There are other problems which have arisen: for example, the growth of anticlerical movements, usually consisting of laymen who oppose any effort of the clergy or the organized church to deal with social issues. They have particularly concerned themselves with opposition to desegregation, to alleged Communism in the churches (often confused with the traditional liberalism of left-of-center political idealism), to the United Nations, and to similar emphases. Such movements often come out of an inadequate understanding of the Christian gospel and reflect the tendency toward religion-in-general

61

discussed in a previous chapter. They tend to be anticlerical rather than concerned with the laity as such, and often are thinly veiled efforts of fundamentalists to discredit the mainline churches.

A great many of our problems grow out of the failure of churchmen to understand in depth the meaning of the Christian gospel. Unless we face up realistically and effectively to this situation, we shall not be likely to actualize the potentiality of the Church as the whole people of God.

There are many signs of renewal within the Church; and although these will be discussed in more detail in a later chapter, this one would be incomplete without brief reference to them. There are unusual examples of parish renewal. There are an increasing number of study and retreat centers to which laymen may go for brief periods of renewal and study. In America the most significant of all is the emergence in many local congregations of the small fellowship and study group in which laymen come to grips with a deepened understanding of the Christian faith.

There are not only these specific examples of lay concern but also an important emphasis on the laity in the ecumenical movement. To some extent this is a reflection of what is happening in the churches, though it is also a factor leading to a new emphasis by them. The very existence of the Department of the Laity of the World Council of Churches is significant, as are the discussions which have occurred under the sponsorship of the Council. This is affecting churches throughout the world, with the younger churches needing it less than either Europe or America.

This chapter has reviewed briefly both the heritage and the problems which the history of the Church presents to one concerned with the rebirth of the laity today. The American churches are in a particularly good position to participate in this rebirth because of their peculiar heritage. Yet they have their problems partly as the result of the cultural forces indicated in the first chapter. We especially need to be alert to the professionalism which has arisen within the churches and to the confusion which often exists between the use of laymen and the laity's being the Church.

There are indications that a revival is beginning not only with respect to the laity but also among the laity. We shall turn in subsequent chapters to considerations which it is hoped may help in giving direction to this concern in the latter half of the twentieth century.

NOTES

1. There is good reason to suspect any *static* conception of apostolic authority, however, such as seems to be the point of view of one of the standard Anglican works, *The Apostolic Ministry: Essays on the History and the Doctrine of Episcopacy*, prepared under the direction of Kenneth E. Kirk (London: Hodder & Stoughton, 1946), especially pp. 119-33, 180-82, 533-34. Anthony Hanson has recently offered a rather thorough rejection of this point of view. See *The Pioneer Ministry: The Relation of Church and Ministry* (Philadelphia: The Westminster Press, 1961), especially Chap. 7.
2. *Clement's First Letter* 44.2, in *Early Christian Fathers*, trans. and ed. Cyril C. Richardson ("The Library of Christian Classics," Vol. I [Philadelphia: The Westminster Press, 1953]), p. 63.
3. Hanson, *op. cit.*, p. 112; see also pp. 109-12.
4. The difference between *episkopoi* and *presbuteroi*, if there was one, is crucial in determining whether or not the New Testament suggests an episcopal form of church government. To answer this question is not our purpose, however.
5. *Clement's First Letter* 40.5, in Richardson, *op. cit.*, p. 62.
6. *To the Trallians* 3.2, in *ibid.*, p. 99.
7. *To the Smyrnaeans* 8.1-2, in *ibid.*, p. 115.
8. Cf. *The Letters of Ignatius, Bishop of Antioch: Introduction*, in *Ibid.*, pp. 76-78.
9. *Adversus Haereses* IV. xxvi.2, quoted in *Early Latin Theology*, trans. and ed. S. L. Greenslade ("The Library of Christian Classics," Vol. V [Philadelphia. The Westminster Press, 1956]), p. 72.
10. *Ibid.* V. xxxiv.3, quoted by George H. William's, "The Ministry of the Ante-Nicene Church (ca. 125-325)," in *The Ministry in Historical Perspectives*, ed. H. Richard Niebuhr and Daniel D. Williams (New York: Harper & Brothers, 1956), p. 36.
11. Hanson, *op. cit.*, p. 117.
12. Williams, *op. cit.*, p. 45.

13. Reinhold Seeberg, *History of Doctrines in the Ancient Church* (Text-Book of the History of Doctrines, Vol. I [Grand Rapids, Mich.: Baker Book House, 1952]), 177.
14. *Constitution of the Holy Apostles* II. iii.xx and II. iv.xxvi, in *The Ante-Nicene Fathers*, ed. Alexander Roberts and James Donaldson (New York: Charles Scribner's Sons, 1899), VII, 404, 410.
15. Roland H. Bainton, "The Ministry in the Middle Ages," in Niebuhr and Williams, *op. cit.*, p. 91.
16. Bainton, *loc. cit.*
17. N. Afanassieff, *op. cit.*, pp. 34-35.
18. *Letter 107: To Laeta*, in *Early Latin Theology*, pp. 330-44.
19. Congar, *op. cit.*, especially pp. 20 ff.
20. Quoted in George Huntston Williams, "The Role of the Layman in the Ancient Church," in *Greek and Byzantine Studies*, ed. John J. Bilitz (P.O. Box 184, Elizabeth, New Jersey), p. 24.
21. Ernst Troeltsch, *The Social Teaching of the Christian Churches*, trans. Olive Wyon (New York: The Macmillan Company, 1931, 1956), I, 350.
22. *Ibid.*, p. 351.
23. *Ibid.*, pp. 354-55. Although the Waldensians still retain their name, they were affiliated with the Reformed wing of the Reformation at the time of the Reformation.
24. For a discussion of Wycliffe, Huss, and the movement stemming from Huss, see *Ibid.*, pp. 358-69.
25. See, for example, Roland H. Bainton, *The Age of the Reformation* (Anvil Books; Princeton, N. J.: Van Nostrand, 1956) and Williston Walker, Rev. by Cyril C. Richardson, Wilhelm Pauck, and Robert T. Handy, *A History of the Christian Church* (Edinburgh: T. & T. Clark, 1959), Period Six, pp. 301-421.
26. Quoted by Wilhelm Pauck, "The Ministry in the Time of the Continental Reformation," from Luther's *Works* (Weimar Edition), VI, 564, in Niebuhr and Williams, *op. cit.*, p. 112.
27. H. Kraemer, *op. cit.*, pp. 64-68.
28. For example, it was Calvin's wish that Holy Communion be celebrated weekly, but after much struggle the magistrates prevailed in favor of a much less frequent celebration. See William D. Maxwell, *An Outline of Christian Worship: Its Development and Forms* (New York: Oxford University Press, 1936, 1955), especially pp. 117-18.
29. This is discussed by Littell in a chapter to be included in a proposed volume edited by Stephen C. Neill under the sponsorship of the Department of the Laity of the World Council of Churches and tentatively entitled *The Laity in Historical Perspective*.
30. Discussed in *ibid.*; see also his *The Free Church* (Boston: Starr King Press, 1957) and Gunnar Westin, *The Free Church Through the Ages*, trans. Virgil A. Olson (Nashville: Broadman Press, 1958).
31. Cf. Littell's chapter noted above. For a brief presentation see his article, "A New View of the Laity," in *Religious Education*, LVI (Jan.-Feb. 1961), 39-44, especially p. 41.
32. *Faith and Practice of the Philadelphia Yearly Meeting of the Religious Society of Friends: A Book of Christian Discipline* (Philadelphia: 1515 Cherry Street, 1955), p. 61.

33. F. C. Mather, for example, presents a rather surprisingly adequate picture of the laity in the Church of England in his chapter of *The Laity in Historical Perspective.*

34. Kraemer, *op. cit.*, p. 17.

35. This will be discussed further in Chap. 6, where additional documentation will be presented.

36. I have developed this theme in more detail in a chapter in *The Laity in Historical Perspective.*

37. James Truslow Adams, *The Rise of the Union* (*The March of Democracy: A History of the United States,* Vol. I [New York: Charles Scribner's Sons, 1932, 1933]), p. 36.

38. Elizabeth H. Davidson, *The Establishment of the English Church in Continental American Colonies; Historical Papers of the Trinity College Historical Society,* Series XX (Durham, N. C.: Duke University Press, 1936), p. 19.

39. H. R. Weber, the Secretary of the Department of the Laity of the World Council of Churches, has concluded that this general emphasis may be one of America's real contributions to the ecumenical movement. See "A Greenhorn's Impression of the People of God in North America," *The Ecumenical Review,* IX (Apr. 1957), 227-28.

40. Robert Baird, *Religion in America. . .* (New York: Harper & Brothers, 1844), p. 132; see also pp. 131-38.

41. William Warren Sweet, *Religion in Colonial America* (New York: Charles Scribner's Sons, 1942), Chap. 7.

42. *Ibid.,* pp. 273-74.

43. Winfred Ernest Garrison and Alfred T. DeGroot, *The Disciples of Christ: A History* (St. Louis: Christian Board of Publication, 1945), p. 341.

44. Edwin Augustine White and Jackson A. Dykman, *Annotated Constitution and Canons for the Government of the Protestant Episcopal Church in the United States of America* (rev. ed.; Greenwich, Conn.: The Seabury Press, 1954), I, pp. 7-8.

45. *Ibid.,* p. 327.

46. I have documented this struggle in an unpublished doctoral dissertation, *Making Lay Leadership Effective: A Historical Study of Major Issues in the Use of Laymen by The Methodist Church Especially for Its Educational Program* (New York: Columbia University, 1949).

47. Henry Steele Commager, *The American Mind: An Interpretation of American Thought and Character Since the 1880's* (New Haven: Yale University Press, 1950), p. 426.

48. See, for example, the recent analysis of the American Baptist Convention by Paul M. Harrison, *Authority and Power in the Free Church Tradition: A Social Case History of the American Baptist Convention* (Princeton, N. J.: Princeton University Press, 1959), especially Chap. 6.

49. Kraemer, *op. cit.*, pp. 165-66.

CHAPTER 4

THE GATHERED CHURCH

Thus far we have looked at the human situation and the failure of organized religion to deal with it adequately. We also briefly surveyed the biblical answer to the human situation—God's forgiveness and grace offered in Christ, made known in and through the new covenant community, the Church—insisting that this is the Word which man needs in his fear and meaninglessness. It was further asserted that a proper understanding of this biblical community must be based on an inclusive view of its constituency—that is, on its reality as the whole people of God. Problems which have arisen in our day, especially in America, were examined not with any desire to be hypercritical but rather in the hope that such an examination may be a factor in the renewal of the Church.

These are the "settings" in which the modern task of the Church must be seen: contemporary life, the biblical faith, historical development. It is our purpose now after having examined these facets of the background to the current situation, to deal more constructively with the issues involved in the Church's again becoming in fact and in deed the whole people of God, able to witness effectively to the One who called it into being.

66

A Theology of the Laity

We have already noted how Father Congar, a Roman Catholic,[1] and Hendrik Kraemer, a Protestant,[2] writing about the nature of the laity, have insisted that there can be no theology of the laity as such but only a theology of the Church which takes into full account its entire membership, including the laity. This we have already done within the context of biblical theology, believing, in fact, that the Church cannot be understood except as it is placed in its larger setting of God's acts in history (revelation) and man's reception of revelation to which the Bible witnesses. It remains for us to look more specifically at what this means functionally for both clergy and laity as they seek to be the Church gathered together as a common people. The scattering of the Church into the world will be considered in the following chapter.

That there are different ways of understanding the ministry of the Church, and thus the laity, we have already briefly noted in Chapter 2. Indeed there are three broad positions, each with variations, which affect the precise way in which we understand the laity.[3] First there is the position characteristic of Roman Catholicism, many Anglicans, some Protestants, and to some extent Eastern Orthodoxy, in which the *esse* (being, reality) of the Church is thought of as entirely or to some extent peculiarly dependent upon the ordained ministry. The argument for this position runs as follows: Jesus called unto himself the apostles—at first the twelve—into whose hands he entrusted a special ministry and which it was their prerogative to pass on to their successors. Thus the Church was first constituted by Christ through his gifts to the apostles which they in turn transmitted to others by the laying on of hands. Ordination as a sacrament confers upon these special ministers a grace (endowment) which then sets them apart as part of the apostolic succession, this being necessary for the full existence of the Church.

Father Congar states this position as held by Roman Catholicism quite clearly when he writes: "Lay people will always form a subordinate order in the Church." [4] Eastern Orthodoxy, while not maintaining this rigid dichotomy between clergy and laity, nevertheless insists that since the laity do "not possess the gifts of government or of teaching," they "cannot be co-ministers of the bishop in the spheres of government and teaching" since the latter receive special gifts "by the sacrament of ordination." [5] This appears to be the view of the Church of Scotland theologian, T. F. Torrance, whose position was discussed in Chapter 2.[6] Norman Pittenger, an Episcopalian, makes a conscious effort to avoid any identification of the Church with the ordained ministry but nevertheless declares that it has an "ontological status" in the Church and that the ordained priest functions "for Christ as Priest in His priestly Church." As James Smart has observed, there is almost no recognition of the continuity of the modern ministry with its prophetic antecedents, only one paragraph being devoted to preaching.[7]

A second position, characteristic of the "free" churches of the left wing of the Reformation and quite common in America, involves quite an opposite view of the esse of the Church. Those who adhere to this view insist that the Church is constituted by the whole people of God—all those called by Christ into his body irrespective of office, with no real distinctiveness for those who make up the set-apart ministry. The more common understanding of how the Church came into being places its origin not in the calling by Jesus of the apostles but in the coming of the Spirit at Pentecost. The primary emphasis is thus not on historic continuity but on the immediate presence of the Spirit; and the authenticity of the Church is attested not by its historic ministry but by the evidence of the presence of the Spirit within a people today. Any special ministry which exists is thus of secondary importance, the result of practical needs and unnecessary even for the well-being (*bene esse*) of the Church. Either such a special ministry is denied, as in the case of the Friends, or is held to a minimum, as in the movement stemming from the Campbells.

Such a view has been summarized by a British Baptist, Arthur Dakin, in a monograph, *The Baptist View of the Church and Ministry*. The separated minister is only one of the members of the church set aside to perform certain functions, and "once he ceases to perform those functions in that particular church, he ceases to be a Baptist minister." [8] The position has also been recently stated by Arnold Come, a Presbyterian, in a less radical way, for while recognizing the existence of a functional division between clergy and laity, he insists that any real division between the two is fundamentally wrong.[9] He would thus eliminate the use of the word "laity" altogether, feeling that it inevitably suggests a state inferior to the clergy. "The church is now ready for, and its God-given mission now demands," he writes, "*the complete abandonment of the clergy-laity distinction.*" [10] The ministry of the Church, which is the proclamation of God's reconciling love, must be seen, as the New Testament views it, as the responsibility of the total Church; [11] and to continue the division between clergy and laity is to thwart God's purposes. It is his contention "that even the most thorough and effective intensification of the active role of the laity will never rid the church of what is now an archaic clericalism." [12] "Maintaining the *diversity* of ministries is just as important as ascertaining that every member shares in the church's ministry," [13] he continues, but this diversity has no place for a twofold ministry suggested by the clergy-laity distinction.

Both of these positions are clear and unequivocal. The first is easily implemented since it places authority clearly in the hands of a special group (usually the bishops) and defines the limitations of the laity in reasonably precise terms. The second is appealing—one which I am continually tempted to assume —but nevertheless difficult to implement as the early church soon learned, as Luther came to see, and as demonstrated by the development of professionalism, in contrast with clericalism, in American Protestantism. So far as I can see, one of the few groups which have maintained, with a few exceptions, the purity of this view is the Friends, which has remained a relatively small group within the total Christian community. Groups such as the Church of the Latter Day Saints (Mormons) have also held essentially to this view.

Thus, although it is more difficult to describe and lacks both the clarity and the simplicity of the other two views, I should like to support a third view which recognizes that the ordained clergy, while not the *esse* of the Church, is nevertheless part of its *bene esse* (well-being). It begins at the same point as the second position, with an insistence that it is the whole people of God whom God calls into being through Jesus Christ. The nature of the ministry, as James Smart insists, "is determined for all time by the ministry of Jesus Christ." [14] The apostles were the original witnesses to his ministry, and as such maintain a unique position in the historic continuity of the Church. Their ministry continued his ministry, not in its precise form, to be sure, but in general substance.[15] For the constitution of the Church in its fullness, it was not only necessary that Christ should continue among them because of the Resurrection but also that he should leave them (the Ascension) and send the Spirit in his name (John 14:18-31). When the Church began is a question we shall not likely determine with any finality, but the experience of Pentecost, with its emphasis on the presence of the Holy Spirit, is at least necessary to understand the fullness of the Church.

To be sure, the exact position of the apostles (the twelve and Paul) is not easy to determine, though it is obvious from the New Testament that they occupied a unique position in the total body. It is they who lay their hands on, "ordain," the deacons in Acts 6:1-6. It is they whom Paul always lists first in the offices of the Church. But the New Testament is strangely silent on the precise relationship between the *apostoloi* (apostles) of the early epistles and the *episkopoi* (bishops) of I Tim. 3:1, the *diakonoi* (deacons) of I Tim. 3:8, and the *presbuteroi* (elders) of I Tim. 5:17. In all of these passages, the important point seems to be that certain offices were singled out for special consideration from the variety of offices and ministries which existed.

The word which is often used to indicate the relationship between the separated ministry and the general ministry of the Church is "representative." Perhaps there is none better; yet it is fraught with difficulties. It is not that the special ministry represents the general ministry before God, nor that the special ministry is subject to the whims of the total ministry, as has sometimes been the case in practice. It is rather the possession by the special ministry of "gifts and graces" which make them able to function *representatively*; that is, in the name of Christ, on behalf of the total ministry of the congregation, their willingness so to function stemming from their response to God's call to service. The ordained minister is, as it were, the link between the Church throughout time and space and the individual congregation.[16] His gifts, graces, special training, and freedom from responsibilities outside the Church make it possible for him to do certain things better than other ministers in the Church. But his set-apartness does not remove him from the *laos tou Theou* (people of God); it only frees him to act in this special capacity. Baptism is the ordination of ministers, and clerical ordination confers no special grace. For the sake of order, the Church has set up such ordination as a means of linking this individual with the tradition of the Church. From this perspective even apostolic succession may be asserted, though I am inclined to believe that it is too often viewed more as a mechanical process than as a means of linking the special ministry to the past. In any case the historic succession must never be viewed as a substitute for the authorization of the special ministry which is attested by

71

the presence of the Spirit. It only need be remembered that "God is not a God of confusion but of peace" (I Cor. 14:33).

It is this position which is assumed, though perhaps not fully enunciated, in Kraemer's *A Theology of the Laity*.[17] It is also maintained by Daniel Jenkins in *The Protestant Ministry*.[18] It is also assumed by Douglas Blatherwick, a British Methodist layman, when he asserts that as a layman he gladly accepts the sacraments from the special ministry and looks to it for leadership.[19] It is, I believe, also the general position maintained by Hans-Ruedi Weber, formerly chairman of the Department of the Laity of the World Council of Churches.[20] It is more fully expounded in James Smart's recent book, *The Rebirth of Ministry*.[21]

To be sure the position has the inherent danger of not going far enough, of continuing the dichotomy between the two major divisions of the ministry. Yet for the sake of order, it seems necessary in contrast to the view which maintains no separateness at all. And because I believe it is basically in keeping with the New Testament doctrine of the ministry and because I believe that the radical separateness which developed within the first two centuries of the church is foreign to the New Testament, I think it must be held in contrast to the first position. It is important to add, however, that the division is necessary provided it is clearly grounded in a view of the Church which makes no *organic* distinction between the orders of clergy and laity.

Ministry as "Service"

What has been said in the previous section is based upon the assumption that the Church is called to service and that this service (*diakonia*) is the responsibility of the entire Church. Or, to use the terminology which has arisen in ecumenical circles, the Church *is* ministry, or the Church *is* mission. The "barb" in I Pet. 2:9 is often overlooked: "But you are a chosen race, a royal priesthood, a holy nation, God's own people, *that you may declare the wonderful deeds of him who called you out of darkness into his marvelous light*" (Italics mine). "There are varieties of gifts," to quote Paul, "but the same Spirit; and there are varieties of service [*diakonion*], but the same Lord." (I Cor. 12:4-5.) An individual is called into the Body of Christ not for special privilege but to use his gifts for the work of ministry.[22] As we have seen, however, it was the temptation of Israel, as it is still the temptation of the Church, to think of special privilege rather than responsibility.

The first response of the Christ is worship of (service to) God. The difficulty of distinguishing between worship and service is indicated by the problem of translating the Greek word *latreian* in Rom. 12:1. In the Septuagint the word was always applied to divine service, and the lexicons are hard put, as are the translators of the New Testament into English, to know whether to use service or worship as the best equivalent.[23] The New English Bible offers something of a paraphrase in its rendition: "Therefore, my brothers, I implore you by God's mercy to offer your very selves to him: a living sacrifice, dedicated and fit for his acceptance, the worship offered by mind and heart." And in the footnote an alternate reading of the final phrase is suggested, "For such is the worship which you, as rational creatures, should offer." [24] One New Testament scholar has suggested this paraphrase: "The offering of one's *self* to God is the only adequate way of worshipping God." [25]

A similar point is made by the meaning of the Greek *leitourgia*, from which the word "liturgy," or "mode of worship," is derived. The literal meaning is "the discharge of a public office at one's own expense," hence "a service ministry."[26] As Dom Gregory Dix has made clear, the liturgy, or divine worship, was originally thought of as something *done*

73

before God [27]—it was man's action before the holy and transcendent God. The Eastern Orthodox tradition has more completely retained this view, at least in theory, insisting that "liturgical acts are performed by the head of the Church with the con-celebration of the laity." [28] It is significant also that the most important way in which the Roman Catholic Church is now seeking to interpret the priesthood of the laity is through their common action in the Mass.[29]

But the mission of the Church has a horizontal as well as a vertical dimension, and the two cannot be separated. Those who find in Paul the denial of the importance of works following faith have failed to take seriously such passages as Rom. 12. I John puts it cogently: "But if any one has the world's goods and sees his brother in need, yet closes his heart against him, how does God's love abide in him?" (I John 3:17.) And Jesus is quoted as putting it quite bluntly: "As you did it to one of the least of these my brethren, you did it to me." (Matt. 25:40b; also 45 for the reverse statement.) Further, he repeatedly interpreted his own vocation and ministry in terms of service, taking the image of the suffering servant in Second Isaiah as that which shaped that ministry: "For the Son of man also came not to be served but to serve, and to give his life as a ransom for many" (Mark 10:45). If, as Smart insists, the character of Jesus' ministry shapes the nature of our ministry, then the basic character of our call seems clear. The call of the Christian to service is the unmistakable and clarion note of the New Testament, matched by the prophet's insistence in the Old Testament that Israel too was called to service.

Thus, any rethinking of the nature of the Church which takes into full account the laity must be matched by the willingness of the laity to assume intelligently and zealously their full responsibility as participant servants among the people of God.

74

Implementing the Laity's Ministry

The ministry of the laity occurs in two separable but interrelated realms, in the Church as called together (as *ekklesia*) and in the world which the Church is called to serve (the laity in *diaspora*). The former is the realm in which both laity and clergy carry on a mutual ministry; the latter, to be considered in the following chapter, is increasingly, in our secularized culture, primarily the work of the laity who live most of their lives in this culture.

We have already noted that the primary service of clergy and laity alike is worship of God. Let us now look at some of the horizontal ministries of the laity as they are gathered together in the Church.

First, but not necessarily of primary importance, is the area of *church government*, the ordering of the inner life of the organized church. Here neither Roman Catholicism nor Orthodoxy gives real prerogatives to the laity, though Orthodoxy, as we have noted, does maintain a modicum of participation in terms of "judgment" and "consent." [30] Such work is reserved for those who have received the special grace conferred by ordination.

In Protestant groups the extent to which the laity governs varies, as we saw in the previous chapter. How much the growth of lay participation in church government reflects the growing democratic milieu in America and how much it represents a genuine appraisal of the nature of the Church is a matter of disagreement. At any rate, as we have suggested, there has existed the danger that the "congregation under God" will become the "congregation as democratically organized and governed." So long, however, as we do not recognize the conveying of special grace through ordination, there appears to be no reason why laymen should be excluded from church governing bodies. It should be noted, however, that both clergy and laity are under the imperative to govern the flock *under*

75

Christ and not according to their whims and fancies. Both are responsible to God ultimately, and neither clergy nor ruling elders are either independent or responsible just to the congregation. A layman who is allowed to control a local congregation, as sometimes happens, is no more exercising his proper ministry than a clergyman who does so. Indeed, our church groups, consisting of both clergy and laity, would be wise to spend more time in prayer and less time in political chicanery.

A second area of lay activity is within the *planning committee structure* of the Church, that is, in those groups responsible for thinking through and planning for the execution of some aspect of the life of the Church.

As an example, consider the Christian Education Committee of a local congregation which, in view of the Protestant emphasis on lay responsibility for the teaching ministry, is often one of the most important of these planning groups. Increasingly such groups are spending a day or two before the beginning of the church-school year, preferably away from telephones and other interferences, thinking through the nature of the Church's teaching ministry and then planning how it may be effectively implemented. Unfortunately, however, regular meetings of such groups still devote too much time to minor details. I remember one group that spent a considerable part of an evening trying to decide whether, and then how, to install a light over the desk of the secretary of a church-school department! Many such details can be left to a committee or to a single person, with the entire group spending its time in thoughtful, prayerful search for a deeper understanding of its work.

For example, many of the denominations have already rethought, or are in process of rethinking, the nature of their curriculum materials. Methodist groups might consider the basic document *Foundations of Christian Teaching in Methodist Churches;*[31] Presbyterian, U. S., groups could spend many hours considering the "Foundation" papers recently issued by its Board of Christian Education;[32] United Presbyterian Churches still need deeper understanding of its "Christian Faith and Life Curriculum," initiated more than ten years ago,[33] there is a wealth of material which Episcopal groups might take into account in understanding the new "Seabury Series"; [34] and those congregations affiliated with the United Church of Christ will need to consider seriously their new curriculum as it is issued step by step.

Unfortunately, especially in larger churches, laymen are often called upon to approve what the national board has done or what the local paid staff has decided, not only in Christian education but also in evangelism and other phases of the life of the Church. They remain the "clergy's little helpers," or perhaps the "directer of Christian education's little helpers." These specially prepared persons have a responsibility, as we shall later see, for guiding the process, but the Church is not really exercising its total priesthood until laymen are involved in policy making as well as detailed matters of implementation.

Third, laymen also serve as *administrators* in the church. An increasing number of larger churches, in fact, are employing laymen full time to assume many of the administrative details which otherwise the pastor must carry out. Apart from such full-time assistants ("business managers" or "executive assistants," as they are somewhat unfortunately designated), there are many part-time administrative posts—superintendents in the church school, committee chairman, officers in youth and adult church-school classes and women's groups, and the like. Such leaders need help in knowing how to be adequate church leaders, the practices which they import from their business experience not always being appropriate in a church setting.

Fourth, the *teaching ministry* of Protestantism is shared by clergy and laity alike. Unlike Roman Catholicism and Orthodoxy, where the clergy or specially prepared lay orders do the

77

teaching, Protestantism has relied largely on the laity since the inception of the Sunday-school movement more than a century and a half ago. There is reason to believe, in fact, that we have relied too much on the laity, with the clergy's refusing their share in this ministry. The quality of the Church's teaching has suffered because the one most prepared to teach (the clergyman, and to some extent the director of Christian education) leaves this to the layman.

There are those in Christian education in this and a previous generation[35] who are convinced that this work cannot be done by volunteer laymen. To be sure, it is asking a great deal of busy lay people for them to assume the responsibilities of teaching Sunday after Sunday; and we are in need of rotation systems for teachers, plans for making it possible for laymen to assume leadership periodically, and other means of making the task less arduous. Further, as we shall see more fully in a later section, we are desperately in need of both parent-teachers and church-school teachers who are more knowledgeable concerning the Christian faith.

In spite of the problems which lay teaching involves, however, I am convinced that the system is in harmony with the Protestant understanding of the Chuch, that lay people ought to be "carriers of the faith" as fully as the clergy. So much teaching occurs through relationships—through introducing children, youth, and adults into the redemptive community of family or organized church, a process in which the volunteer layman is likely to be more effective than the professional teacher—that the system seems not only worth preserving but necessary if the view of the Church which has been described is fully implemented. We cannot, however, afford to be complacent about the need for more adequately prepared teachers for both church and family.

Fifth, the *pastoral oversight* of church members can also be partly a lay responsibility. The Church already recognizes this to some extent: laymen as teachers visit their church-school class members, or members their fellow class members; the every member financial campaign involves lay visitors; laymen visit to enlist others in church-school teaching; and so on. Further, there is the informal, unplanned visitation by members to one another in times of crisis, illness, or trouble. The care which the church fellowship exercises at the time of death has not, fortunately, completely disappeared, even in urban communities. A few churches have gone a step further and have systematized their lay pastoral care. For example, a widow of a few months' duration may be assigned to look after a recent widow; a cured alcoholic may assume responsibility for an uncured one; and so on. One of the ways in which the koinonia of which the New Testament speaks may come into being is through such person-to-person ministries.

By and large, however, we have given little help to such persons in their work, assuming at least by default that such personal shepherding requires nothing beyond goodwill. Seward Hiltner is right when he points to the need for some kind of elementary instruction in many aspects of shepherding, with the pastor being the overseer of the entire flock, including those who assume these special responsibilities.[36] It may be, in fact, that the pastor, by working with a group of laymen, can help them be better pastors for certain people than he can be himself. In one congregation I know, the pastor has built up a large group of former alcoholics who perform such a pastoral ministry to other alcoholics. Although the chief pastor does have a particular responsibility here, the work of the laity ought to be more than their assisting him, for all Christians may be surrogates for, or assistants to, the one great Shepherd, or, to use Albert Outler's phrase, they may become good sheep dogs! [37]

Sixth, in addition to this general kind of pastoral oversight, there are laymen in most congregations who can proffer their special gifts to assist other members of the congregation. Psychiatrists are sometimes made available at a reduced fee

to those unable to pay regular prices for specialized psycho-
therapy, and other professional persons may be kept on a
referral basis by a congregation. These same persons—all
those who deal personally with other people—may also be
helped to see the potentialities of their professional compe-
tency as part of the total pastoral outreach of the Church,[38]
though at this point we are dealing more specifically with the
Church in dispersion, which is the subject of the following
chapter.

Seventh, layman also engage in various forms of *service
projects* as part of the organized life of the congregation.
(In some ways this too belongs in the subsequent chapter,
and it is included here only because this is work carried out
through the organized life of the congregation.) Here is a
church-school class that occasionally has a "work party" to do
some piece of work at a mission sponsored by the parent
church. At other times they spend an evening reconditioning
the play equipment in the church nursery. Or here is a group
of young people who visit shut-ins, plan a worship service for
a home for older adults, or clean the church grounds. Here is
a group of unmarried women who serve as sponsors for older
women in the church and community, and another which
helps in transporting older adults to church meetings. Here
is a women's group that provides child care at the church for
the children of working mothers, thus giving to the children
something of the quality of family life while they are separated
from their mothers.

Some of the most faithful and loving service I have known
has been given by women in the kitchen who prepare meals
for church meetings. One woman I know who engaged in this
kind of service for many years has since been struck by partial
paralysis, and since then she carries on her ministry by her
cheerful approach to those who visit her in a nursing home. A
friend of mine recently said that he thought one of the most
unfortunate things about a church in which he was tempo-

rarily employed was the fact that the members almost invariably asked, when some form of service was requested, "Can't we pay someone to do that?"

The choir member who faithfully attends rehearsals and is regularly present to assist in the leading of public worship is performing a more glamorous type of service but one nonetheless needed. I know a woman whose sight is so nearly gone that she can do very little, but she can see well enough to send out cards to sick members of her church-school class. I remember also a faithful church-school secretary who spent long hours making sure that records were adequate and accurate; and though my inherent dislike for keeping records made me fail always to see the relevance of his meticulousness, I could not help appreciating his devotion. There are women who wash and iron the altar linen, who carefully embroider vestments, who assist in the preparation of Communion elements, who do the many unnoticed little acts of service which are necessary for the ongoing life of the congregation.

These are the "deacons" who accepted menial service so that the apostles might not be forced to give up their call to preach the word and serve at tables (Acts 6:2). And through this common work together, there may emerge a spirit of fellowship which could never develop apart from the exercising by the congregation of their several ministries as members of the Body of Christ (I Cor. 12:28-30).

Eighth, some churches make provision for *special lay work*. There is, for example, the lay reader in the Episcopal Church: that is, laymen who, under the direction of the bishop, conduct services of morning and evening prayer and lead other services. In 1960 there were 15,044 such lay readers in the Episcopal Church in the United States, the figure just about having doubled during the preceding decade.[39] In Methodism the lay speaker has recently arisen to take the place of the previously more common "local preacher" and "exhorter" with a similar function. Lay preaching is not uncommon in many communions, and the layman called upon to address numerous church meetings may exercise an influence theologically comparable to that of the separated minister.

This brief description of some forms of lay work within the churches will serve to indicate the breadth of possibilities for lay service within the *ekklesia*. Indeed, as we shall again observe in the subsequent chapter, some lay people become so enmeshed in the life of their local congregation that they neglect their parental responsibilities and have little energy left to bear their witness to the world outside the church. Every local congregation ought to examine periodically the manner in which it assigns duties to lay people, to make sure that no one person is carrying more than a single major responsibility. Not only will this free persons for a more adequate witness in family and society; it will also enlarge the number of those who are active participants in the interior life of the Church.

The Full-Time Church Worker

What, then, is the work of the full-time church worker, ordained or lay? No consideration of the laity is complete without a correlative look at the clergy and other set-apart ministers in the church. Their work is of three main orders:

First, there are *those responsibilities which ordination conveys to the ordained.* For example, the Methodist ritual for the ordination of elders (the fully ordained clergy) contains these words: "Take thou authority as an elder in the Church to preach the Word of God, and to administer the holy Sacraments in the congregation." [40] With a few exceptions most churches reserve to those set aside for the special ministry certain unique responsibilities, the most common being preaching and the administration of the sacraments and the ordinances. So far as I can see there is no reason why this should not be the case. Just as the judge is authorized to preside over a court

82

and the doctor is licensed to practice medicine, so the clergy-man is authorized to preside over the Lord's table and administer baptism. Whether or not laymen assist, as in many churches, is a different question.

Second, there are also various types of work which set-apart ministers do by virtue of their special preparation. It is not possible to deny the validity of the "specialist" in the congregation, both in the clerical and the lay ministry. The danger is when the ministry as such comes to be thought of as the specialized activity. To maintain diverse orders within the total ministry is, of course, quite in harmony with the New Testament.

The principal pastor, for example, is expected to act as a kind of co-ordinator–supervisor for the total life of the church, and it is doubtful whether the occasional practice of making a lay assistant completely responsible for this work is advisable. This is what Richard Niebuhr implies in his rather unfortunate designation of the modern clergyman as "pastoral director." [41] Unfortunately the administration of the kinds of organization which modern churches have become tends to be a full-time job, and the pastor is often hindered by it from doing an adequate job of preparation for his preaching and teaching. A reexamination of church programs might well lead to changes in their emphases; and in large churches the specialized administrative assistant, working with the pastor, may be a solution.

The clergy are also given special training in pastoral work and counseling. Their theological education prepares them for teaching on a deeper level than most laymen are prepared for. It may be that the local congregation ought to become a sort of "theological seminary for laymen" with the pastor as the chief instructor because of his specialized preparation in the theological disciplines.

There are, of course, other specialized ministries in larger churches: the director of Christian education, the counselor-

83

pastor, the associate pastor in charge of evangelism, the organist and choir director, and so on. Such persons together may be designated as a "team ministry," each doing his specialized work but clearly as members of a team of set-apart ministers, all together united by their common concern for the Body of Christ.

Two dangers may arise in this growth of the multiple staff. One is due to an individual's thinking of his work as a separate and distinct activity. Too often in the early days of the development of the specialized worker in Christian education, he and his work were relegated to a position outside of or peripheral to the major work of the church. Sometimes this was the fault of the principal pastor, but the specialized worker was also at times to blame. A second danger, more insidious than the first, occurs when either specialist or congregation or both think of the specialist as doing the work of the congregation. He is, as we shall see, primarily a helper of the congregation as it performs its ministry.

Thus we move to a third—and in many ways the most important—aspect of the responsibility of the set-apart ministry: *to prepare the congregation for its work of ministry.* This is put quite cogently in Eph. 4 if a comma is omitted (and the Greek seems to indicate that it should never have been placed there). The New English Bible, omitting the offending comma, translates the statement in this fashion: "And these were his gifts: some to be apostles, some prophets, some evangelists, some pastors and teachers, to equip God's people for work in his service, to the building up of the body of Christ" (Eph. 4:12).[42] "For the equipment of the saints for the work of ministry" is the Revised Standard Version without the comma, while the King James Version, without the comma, reads, "for the perfecting of the saints for the work of the ministry." The saints are those whose gifts are not included in the previous list. Those with special gifts, both lay and clergy, are to prepare the whole congregation for its work of ministry.

84

Instead of the layman's being the clergyman's little helper, the clergyman, or the director of Christian education, becomes the layman's little helper!

One clear example is seen in the teaching ministry. Niebuhr's analysis of the pastor's role as "teacher or teachers" may seem a bit narrow, for as theologian of the congregation he himself ought to do a maximum amount of teaching to the entire church. Yet the basic idea is sound: the pastor and other members of a team ministry are to pay particular attention to their work of teaching the parent-teachers, the church-school teachers, and the evangelists of the congregation.

Similarly the choir master is to help the choir develop its ministry through music, not to "put on" a performance! The youth director is to develop lay adult leadership for young people—but how often he too "puts on a program" for young people only to have it collapse when he leaves because he has developed no local leadership for the program. The minister of evangelism is to develop lay evangelists, and so on down the list. In some ways, though it will probably never happen, the set-apart ministry, except for those functions reserved to the ordained, ought to have as its goal the eventual demise of their offices!

Unfortunately the special ministry sometimes finds itself acting as a buffer between the higher echelons of church organization and the laity, trying to soften the blow as much as possible when program and statistical demands are made from "higher up." Yet it must be remembered that these "drives," goals, and imposed programs are to some extent the result of the failure of local laity to be a live, dynamic community of the Spirit. Although such artificial means of compelling a local congregation to be about its business may actually at times get in the way of its doing so, they may also remind a group of people that they are responsible before God. And they need not stand in the way of a congregation's becoming "alive in Christ Jesus" when the special ministry sees as its work the equipping of the saints—all of them who will respond—for their ministry in local church and world.

The whole Church in mission—this is the command of the Lord of the Church. But its mission is not just in terms of its interior life; it is also in the world. So in the next chapter we shall turn to what some are now saying is the more important mission of the Church: that the laity shall live responsibly before God as they meet their neighbors in the larger culture in which they work and live.

NOTES

1. Congar, op. cit.
2. Kraemer, op. cit., especially pp. 74 ff.
3. Cf. Paul Rowntree Clifford, The Pastoral Calling (Greak Neck, N. Y.: Channel Press, 1961), pp. 11 ff.
4. Congar, op. cit., p. xxvii.
5. Afanassieff, op. cit., p. 34.
6. Torrance, op. cit., pp. 28 ff.
7. W. Norman Pittenger, The Church, the Ministry, and Reunion (Greenwich, Conn.: The Seabury Press, 1957), especially pp. 14-15, 109, 129, and passim. The comments are not made without appreciation for the attempt which the writer makes toward a conciliatory position. Smart's critique is found in The Rebirth of Ministry (Philadelphia: The Westminster Press, 1960), p. 67 and passim. See also The Apostolic Ministry, op. cit.
8. Quoted in Clifford, op. cit., p. 19; see also p. 20.
9. From Agents of Reconciliation by Arnold B. Come. © 1960, W. L. Jenkins. The Westminster Press. By permission.
10. Ibid., p. 99 (italics his).
11. Ibid., especially pp. 72 ff.
12. Ibid., p. 101.
13. Ibid., p. 105.
14. Smart, op. cit., pp. 29 ff.
15. Ibid., p. 37.
16. I am indebted to Albert C. Outler of the faculty of Perkins School of Theology for help at this point, from a lecture presented before the Field Education groups at Perkins School of Theology, Dallas, Texas, during the fall semester, 1960-61.
17. See especially Chap. 5 in Kraemer, op. cit.
18. Daniel Jenkins, The Protestant Ministry (Garden City, N. Y.: Doubleday & Company, Inc., 1958), especially pp. 34-39.
19. Douglas P. Blatherwick, A Layman Speaks (London: The Epworth Press, 1959), especially pp. 28-31.

20. See, for example, "The Laity in the Apostolic Church," in *A Symposium on the Laity*, pp. 61-68.
21. Smart, *op. cit.*, especially Chaps. 1 and 2.
22. Cf. Come, *op. cit.*, pp. 77-85; Kraemer, *op. cit.*, Chap. 5.
23. See, for example, G. Abbott-Smith, *A Manual Greek Lexicon of the New Testament* (Edinburgh: T. & T. Clark, 1921, 1956), p. 265.
24. *The New English Bible: New Testament*, (Oxford University Press, Cambridge University Press, 1961), p. 272.
25. Suggested to me by Fred D. Gealy, formerly of Perkins School of Theology, Dallas, Texas, now of the Methodist Seminary in Ohio, Delaware, Ohio.
26. Abbott-Smith, *op. cit.*, pp. 266-67.
27. Dom Gregory Dix, *The Shape of the Liturgy* (Naperville, Ill.: Alec R. Allison, 1960), especially Chaps. 1 and 2. See also my *The Church Redemptive*, *op. cit.*, Chap. 6.
28. Afanassieff, *op. cit.*, p. 34.
29. Cf. James Edward Rea, *The Common Priesthood of the Members of the Mystical Body: An Historical Survey of the Heretical Concepts of the Doctrine as Compared with the True Catholic Concept* (Westminster, Md.: Newman Bookshop, 1947), especially Part II, Chap. 4.
30. Afanassieff, *op. cit.*, pp. 35-37.
31. *A Statement of the Curriculum Committee of the General Board of Education of The Methodist Church* (Editorial Division, 201 Eighth Avenue, South, Nashville 3, Tennessee, 1960).
32. "Foundation Papers," nine in number, published by the Board of Christian Education, Presbyterian Church in the United States, and Board of Education, Reformed Church in America (Box 1176, Richmond 9, Virginia, 1960, 1961); also the "Principles" papers.
33. For example, "Basic Principles: Christian Faith and Life" (Board of Christian Education of the Presbyterian Church in the U.S.A., 1947), and "Christian Faith and Life at a Glance" (1956).
34. Including the series of six basic books, *The Church's Teaching* (Greenwich, Conn.: The Seabury Press).
35. See, for example, Wesner Fallaw, *Church Education for Tomorrow* (Philadelphia: The Westminster Press, 1960), especially Chaps. 5-7.
36. Hiltner, *Preface to Pastoral Theology* (Nashville: Abingdon Press, 1958), pp. 37-38.
37. In the lecture cited above.
38. Hiltner, *op. cit.*, pp. 38-39.
39. Walter Herbert Stowe, *More Lay Readers Than Clergy: A Study of the Office of Lay Reader in the History of the Church* (Church Historical Society Publications, No. 42, 1954), p. 26. The 1960 figure is from the office of the National Council of the Protestant Episcopal Church.
40. *Doctrines and Discipline of The Methodist Church, 1960* (Nashville: The Methodist Publishing House, 1960), p. 580.
41. Niebuhr, Williams, and Gustafson, *op. cit.*, pp. 79-94.
42. *Op. cit.*, p. 332.

CHAPTER 5

THE LAITY IN DISPERSION

In the previous chapter we considered the responsibilities of both the general and the special ministries within the redemptive fellowship itself. The two, it was pointed out, interlock and supplement each other, and together contribute to the building up of the Body of Christ. Although only God can bring the redemptive community into being, the response of persons as they mutually minister one to another is one of God's ways of bringing to actuality the potentiality of the fellowship of faith. The Church is a believing community of persons united together in common service under the lordship of Christ.

Here is the laity in *ekklesia*, called out of the world to be God's people. But the temptation of any self-conscious group is for it to become ingrown and exclusive; this was true of Israel and it is still true of the Church. It is the tendency of monasticism and also of the modern small study and fellowship group which will be discussed in a later chapter. It can be seen in the sect groups, especially in their feeling that they have a monopoly on the truth. Indeed it is often when the Church is most deeply conscious of its call from God that it is likely to fall into spiritual pride, which is yet another illustration of the persistence of original sin.

There is, of course, a need for withdrawal and retreat—for the alternation between work and worship, witness and prayer, action and study, life lived in the world and life lived apart from the world. The dangers inherent in the fellowship group do not invalidate such a group. It is necessary, however, that retreat be directed toward the life of the world; that the self-conscious group be made aware of the life beyond; that the common meal be seen as equipping one for the common life.

In modern times we have often put undue emphasis on the laity's time in *ekklesia* in a different way. We have loaded the faithful ones with so many jobs that they are at the church every night for a meeting, thus often neglecting their responsibilities as parents. We have used their energies so fully in the work of the organized church that they have little inclination left to witness in the world. We have too often contributed to the common understanding that "church work" is that done in the church building, or at least clearly in line with its organizational life.

The Dispersed Laity

Within recent years, however, there has appeared a growing emphasis in church life on the necessity of the laity's being the Church in the world, of living Christianly and actively witnessing to their faith in those realms of culture outside the corporate life of the Church. It is not fair, of course, to say that this has not been characteristic of earlier times. Generally, however, it has been thought of as the Christian responding individually and has not been identified with the Church as such. A new dimension is given to daily life when it is interpreted not just as one's individual acts but also as involving, through individual acts, the life of the Body of Christ, the Church.

A Greek word has sometimes been used to indicate the

89

nature of the work, and though it may be a questionable use, it nevertheless is illuminating. This is the word *diaspora,* or the scattering abroad, in contrast with *ekklesia,* or the assembling together. It was the word applied to the Jews whenever they were away from their homeland, which bore for them many of the same characteristics which the corporate life of the Church does for us. In captivity, in the Greco-Roman world —wherever they went—they were the chosen people in dispersion. They did not lose their identity in spite of hostile environments.

There was always a kind of curse attached to being out of the homeland, for among other things the temple was there and this was the place of worship. Further, there was the danger of contamination from the Gentile world. Yet in the Roman world the Jews living outside Palestine built synagogues, attracted Gentiles to their faith, made proselytes out of a few, and made "God-fearers" out of many more. The latter were they who, though attracted to Jewish monotheism and ethical ideals, did not find it possible to accept the ceremonial law, such a person as Cornelius in Acts 10. It is probable that these God-fearers may have provided one of the major sources for the early converts to Christianity. Thus what had been considered a curse was turned into a means by which the world was blessed.

The Acts of the Apostles provides another illustration of how the dispersal of Christians may be a means by which the faith is spread. Following each persecution there was a scattering of the faithful to a larger territory, and "Those who were scattered went about preaching the word" (Acts 8:4). Again, "Those who were scattered because of the persecution that arose over Stephen traveled as far as Phoenicia and Cyprus and Antioch, speaking the word to none except the Jews." (Acts 11:19.) But the spreading influence of the gospel could not be held for Jews only, and "There were some of them, men of Cyprus and Cyrene, who on coming to Antioch spoke to the Greeks also, preaching the Lord Jesus" (11:20). These, of course, were not professional clergymen holding mass meetings, but individuals witnessing to the faith that had caught them up into new meaning and had brought salvation to them.

There is something of a curse attached to the sincere Christian's living his life outside the Christian fellowship. To be sure many church members see so little difference in the world and the Church that they fail to feel the tension of living in two realms. But for those who do see the conflict, it must be endured; and in doing so the Christian is afforded his best opportunity to be an evangelist, to be the Church in the world which God loves.

This witness must be carried on primarily by laymen. To this, all those who have examined the mission of the laity agree. Father Congar, in stating his understanding of the Roman Catholic position, writes that the laity finds its particular vocation in the "Church's earthly phase." Their calling is "to fulfill the Church's mission, in and through engagement in temporal tasks." [1] "Since the Church's apostolic mission," he continues, "carries with it, beyond its purely spiritual duties, influence upon temporal civilization, it follows that this mission is *fully* exercised only through the lay people doing their own proper part in it." [2]

Kraemer expresses an almost identical point of view:

If the laity of the Church, dispersed in and through the world, are really what they are called to be, the real uninterrupted dialogue between Church and world happens through them. They form the daily repeated projection of the Church into the world. They embody the meeting of Church and world.[3]

Arnold Come, who begins his argument at the point of the centrality of God's reconciling message in Christ as the heart of the gospel, sees Christians as "agents of reconciliation" in the world: "The ministry of reconciliation is accomplished by

91

the whole Christian community as its members live and act in every walk of life in the world." [4]

This has likewise consistently been one of the major emphases of the work done by and under the auspices of the Department of the Laity of the World Council of Churches.[5] Similarly this outward thrust of the laity has been among the most important contributions of the "lay centers" in Europe, especially through their concern with the relation of the gospel and daily work.[6]

This point of view is not only sound theologically; it is necessary practically. Particularly in Europe is there such a division between the clergy and the people generally that the former are immediately under suspicion by the latter. It has been found, for example, that often people with no special interest in the Church will come to homes and public buildings to discuss their problems with church people, whereas they would not under any circumstances enter a church building. The presence of a clergyman in such groups tends to stop discussion immediately.[7] Although the situation may be less acute in most parts of the United States, this is not so in all areas. Even in those sections of the country where the church is accepted as a part of the culture and clergymen have retained a degree of respect outside the church, there is often difficulty of communication between clergy and laity. As a single example, the survey of a Midwestern youth community some years ago indicated a discouraging absence of real understanding between the two groups.[8] Other surveys have not done a great deal to dispel the general impression of this one.

There have been, and should continue to be, experiments which attempt to bridge the gap between the clergy and the world. The "worker priest" movement in Europe, in which priests in civilian clothes worked in the factory during the week, was an attempt in this direction. The East Harlem Protestant Parish—and its offspring in other cities—are partially efforts by which clergymen attempt to identify them-

selves with the real daily problems of slum dwellers in such
a manner that they come into a personal relationship with the
people. The industrial church centers in Germany and Britain
are similar movements. The efforts which theological schools
are making to help their students understand the culture in
which they live and work are also in the direction of effecting
a closer relationship between clergy and people.

All of this is likely to be relatively ineffective, however, if
for no other reason than this: most of the work of witness
must be on a person-to-person basis, and the number of clergy
in relation to the laity is too small for much to happen. If the
Church is to make an impact on the world, it must do so
through those whose life and work are carried on in the world
—and these are the Church's laity.

We are, of course, far from the actualization of this point
of view. For one thing the laity within the Church share
in the dilemmas of modern man as described in Chapter 1,
and thus they are not always sure themselves of the message
they are asked to proclaim. Further, they are even more clearly
involved in the domestication of the Christian faith which
has occurred in the process of cultural adaptation by the
Church and the development of "religion-in-general." Although the clergy are saved to some extent from the exigencies of the world, they too are conditioned by it, and the
proclamation of the Gospel from the pulpit has often been
more like a pitchpipe than the call of a bugle.

However bleak the picture may be, and however great is
the need for "new life in the Church," [9] we cannot stop short
of a radical understanding of the responsibility of the Church
for the world. That the Church continually stands under the
judgment of God—and is even now—is one of the cardinal
beliefs of Protestantism. That individual Christians are both
reconciled and being reconciled to God is a truism. That the
Church corporately and that churchmen individually are in
need of the call to repentance and a deepened faith is without

question. That call is being made today through an insistence that the whole people of God must accept their summons from God to act responsibly in the culture in which they live. And unless the call is heeded, it may well be, as Paul Tillich fears, the end of the Protestant era, and God may be forced to choose another agency for his work in the world.

Thus in this emphasis on the laity in dispersion we are not dealing with lofty idealism; rather we are concerned with a realistic necessity: either the laity must respond more fully, or the work of Christ will not be done in our time.

Christian Vocation

But how can the Church work of the laity be implemented in the world? The kinds of activities described in the previous chapter are sufficiently familiar, at least to American readers, that one might almost apologize for listing them. With respect to the laity in *diaspora*, however, the situation is different. Indeed one can be neither final nor particularistic in suggestions made in this area of concern. Three overarching concepts do give direction to the inquiry, however: Christian vocation, Christian service, and Christian witness. To the first of these we now turn.

Like many New Testament concepts, the meaning of "Christian vocation" has been obscured, having been often identified with full-time church work. Yet the basic New Testament words, *klesis* (calling) and *kletos* (called) normally refer to the general call of God to man, only occasionally to the call to some office.[10]

Eph. 4:1 may serve as a single example of the broader use: "I therefore, a prisoner for the Lord, beg you to lead a life worthy of the calling [*kleseos*] to which you have been called [*eklethete*]." (See also Rom. 11:29; I Cor. 1:26; Eph. 1:18; Phil. 3:14, and Heb. 3:1.) Our calling is the summons to faith in Christ and to service in faith. "There is one vocation (call)

94

for all, yet each has his own distinctive work to do," writes the New Testament scholar, Paul Minear. "Wherever present labor does not advance his vocation, that labor is sinful and futile." [11]

The more restricted use of the word is less common. When Paul uses the term in Romans and I Corinthians, we cannot always be sure whether he is using it in a specific or a general sense; that is, to refer to the general call to all Christians or the call to an office. Further, in one case he uses it still differently: to denote the state or station in life in which one finds one's self. "Every one should remain in the state [*klesei*] in which he was called [*eklethe*]." (I Cor. 7:20.) [12] Following this lead, Luther used the German word *Beruf* to indicate the state of the Christian in which he is to serve. A calling to him was a station in life which is helpful to others and which may consist not only of an occupation but also of a relationship, like fatherhood and motherhood. Nothing we do which concerns the world or our neighbor "falls in a private sphere lying outside of station, office, or vocation." [13]

In the broadest sense, then, our vocation is to serve God in all of life. But how do we serve him? It is largely through these "stations" in life that we touch the lives of others—as parents, neighbors, friends, workmen, politicians, and so on. Although it is not alone through our daily work that we exercise our call, there is a special sense in which we do so in that area, since so much of our lives are spent in our occupations— as lawyer, doctor, manual laborer, skilled craftsmen, housewife, domestic servant, student, serviceman.

One of the "stations" in which some persons fulfill their calling is through full-time church work, either as an ordained or a lay worker. Some groups have placed a great deal of emphasis on the special call to such service, identified by Richard Niebuhr as the "secret call." [14] Recently some have denied categorically the distinctiveness of such a call, zealous as they are to assert the biblical doctrine of vocation.[15] In view of

95

Paul's consciousness of his own call to apostleship, however, there seems to be neither contradiction nor inconsistency in the two emphases so long as one holds to the position that the set-apart ministry, while having a character of its own, is nevertheless derived from the general ministry. The general call comes first, the special call second. Further, as Niebuhr indicates, the special call must be verified by the "providential call" ("gifts and graces" for the set-apart ministry) and the "ecclesiastical call" (the Church's validation and implementation of the secret call).[16] Nothing, however, must be allowed to obscure or minimize the importance of the general vocation of the whole Church and its members to serve God in the world; and thus we must continue to struggle against a view of Christian vocation which restricts it to full-time church work.

It is not difficult to see how many occupations other than full-time church work provide a natural setting for the exercise of the divine call. For example, the medical doctor has unlimited opportunities for service to his fellow men.[17] Nor is it a problem to discern the possibilities of Christian service through teaching, nursing, social work, and similar "service" professions. It is not so easy to see the Christian possibilities in selling, engineering, manual labor, assembly-line work, and other such occupations. Our problem, however, is that we insist upon an obvious service motif rather than accepting all useful work as a gift from God through which man's energies can be channeled. Our thinking is so permeated with a hierarchy of values in occupations—such as Thomas Aquinas set out in the Middle Ages—that only a radical acceptance of the world as God's world and all useful work as a gift from God can change our thinking.

There are, of course many questions relating to the Christian and his daily work which we are only beginning to answer, though the series of books currently under way by Association

Press on the various occupations is a step in the right direction.[18] For example, does all work qualify under the heading
"useful"? Most of us would want to remove those types of
work which are obviously harmful to mankind, though we
are not always in agreement as to what is harmful. Many Protestants would exclude the dealer in alcoholic beverages even
though their practices in the purchase of such beverages often
indicate an opposite view. Certainly all would agree that deal-
ers in obvious pornography, in prostitution, and in narcotics
should be excluded.

But what about the scientist who perfects the weapons
capable of destroying human life, perhaps all mankind?
What about the advertising firm that misrepresents a product,
or has as its purpose the "hidden persuasion" [19] of persons to
buy products they do not necessarily need or even want?
What about selling practices which have as their aim to
manipulate the purchaser into the buying of an automobile
that he neither can afford nor maximally utilize? Can a
politician be elected to public office by adhering to principles,
especially if those principles are counter to cultural forces
(such as opposition to desegregation in the South)?

Further, there is the whole problem of the monotony of
much modern labor. Is there any way by which a worker on an
assembly line can find meaning in his daily work? And what
about those who are forced to remain in work they despise
because no alternative is available? There are many un-
answered questions relative to the exercise of God's call in
daily work.

Nor can answers be given simply and categorically in our
complex culture. In a subsequent chapter we shall consider a
means for carrying on the kind of interchange which will help
solve the problem; namely, the study group met together on
the basis of occupation to consider the relevance of the Christian faith to problems that participants face in their daily

97

work. Only in this way are the complex issues of our culture likely to be faced realistically; and only as they are faced by those actively engaged in the problems themselves is there much hope that the laity will be helped to live Christianly in the face of such issues. The answer is not necessarily—as the clergy is wont to advise—that a person leave an occupation, though this may be the solution; this, however, may be only another way of withdrawing from the world. The answer more often lies in the willingness to struggle amidst the contingencies and particularities of human existence in an effort to be a transforming influence within these difficult occupations. The support of other struggling human beings is a necessary requisite for the task.

Christian Service

A second motif, as old as the Christian message itself, is Christian service. As we have indicated previously, such service is made the basis for judgment in Jesus' picture of the Last Judgment (Matt. 25:31-46). It is dramatically emphasized in I John 3:17 and throughout this letter where service to fellow men is interrupted, as it is in Matt. 25, as service to God. Paul's emphasis on justification by grace through faith was never intended to be an excuse for an unconcern for the neighbor, as I Cor. 13, along with many other passages, clearly indicates. As we have said, the New Testament meaning of ministry is *diakonia,* or service.

Unfortunately in our complex world, service is not always as simple as giving a cup of water or rescuing the victim of a robbery, as in the parable of the good Samaritan in Luke 10:29-37. Such service to one's own family, immediate neighbors, and personal friends is possible, and we may rejoice that the rural practice of taking food to a sick friend (as a single example) is not entirely absent from our urban, industrial society.

98

But such personalized acts of love and concern are only a partial fulfillment of the command to love our neighbor.

A professor of mine in seminary[20] used this homely but pertinent illustration to indicate the inadequacy of giving the cup of water. The Church, he insisted, has always been willing to have an ambulance at the bottom of a cliff to minister to the needs of those who fall off the cliff. It has been much less willing to build a fence at the top of the cliff to prevent people from falling off. This was his way of insisting that the Church must enter actively into the world, seeking to encourage the doing of those things which contribute to the development of communities, nations, and a world conducive to the welfare of persons.

George Webber, in his book based on the work of the East Harlem Protestant Parish in New York City, has made this point with telling force. Don Benedict, the first full-time clergyman in the parish, happened to see a truck driver run a red light and seriously injure an old man. The instinctive impulse of the "good Samaritan" is to put the man in his car and rush him to the hospital. But in New York City, as in most cities, to do so might involve all kinds of problems, especially if in the moving of the man he was further injured. So Benedict did what he should have done: he called an ambulance and waited beside the man until it arrived, an hour and thirty-seven minutes later.[21] As Webber observes, "The only way really to fulfill the biblical injunction would be to get better ambulance service for East Harlem." [22] Although he does not go on to say this, another step might well be to secure better police regulation of traffic so that ambulances are less necessary.

The specter of the "social gospel" movement haunts us when we begin to discuss what has often been called "social action." That movement, as sincere as its leaders and adherents were, naïvely assumed that the kingdom of God could be

99

brought in by social pronouncements and welfare legislation and that the organized church was responsible for exerting pressure to secure such measures. We still have such pronouncements, many of which unnecessarily antagonize laymen against councils of churches and church legislative bodies. There is, I believe, a place for the church body, denominational or interdenominational, to speak to the church membership on social issues, but the end result is sometimes to hinder rather than help because the laity has not been prepared for the reception of the pronouncement.

What Webber is talking about and what is intended here is the actual working on social issues either by individual Christians through their corporate responsibilities or by groups of concerned Christians co-operating together. He records, for example, in some detail how the parish handled the matter of drug addiction in East Harlem: through the presentation on vacant lots in the community of a play dealing with dope addiction; through the providing of counseling for addicts and their families; and through working with city officials on matters of legislation and enforcement.[23] Elsewhere I have described in some detail how a group of Christian, Jewish, and Unitarian laymen, mostly women, worked toward changing the climate of opinion in Dallas, Texas, with respect to the United Nations.[24]

That laymen can become concerned over social issues is demonstrated by current campaigns, many of them harmful, to acquaint the public with the dangers of Communism. These campaigns are harmful because they fail to get at the heart of the problem—self-examination and repentance on the part of the Church—and because they indiscriminatedly include social liberals with Communists, and resort to methods of hysteria and fright without having any constructive program into which to channel useful efforts. In a way, however, the churches must be blamed for the hysteria, because of their failure to consider realistically and on a broad basis a problem of concern to most Americans.

The service which ameliorates and deals with immediate human need and the action which seeks to get at the causes of such need must not, if they are to be distinctly Christian, be performed under secular motives, but rather under the Christian command to love one's neighbor. Webber quite rightly discusses such matters under a section headed "The Love of Christ, Freely Given." [25] It should be clear also that such work cannot be done solely, or even primarily, by the clergy. One of the unfortunate aspects of the social gospel movement was that it was clerically dominated, and the laity were not carried along in its concerns.

There are many obstacles in the way of laymen's becoming concerned over human needs, especially when the answer given must be in the form of political action. The social conservatism of middle-class churchmen may stand in the way of constructive social action, especially when such action challenges the present structures of society. Yet there are often areas of agreement, and social liberals must be open to solutions not necessarily connected with efforts of the government—local, state, or federal—just as conservatives must not automatically reject governmental solutions to problems that are too complex to be handled adequately through private means. It should be added, moreover, that public solutions have been increasingly necessary, partly because Christian laymen have refused to work on the problems on a private level.

As in the discussion of Christian vocation, it must be noted that our prime need now is for serious considerations by groups of clergy and laity as to how the love of Christ can be best implemented in our complex society. The means for doing this is through the group met together in the Spirit of Christ, open to the leading of the Spirit as members together wrestle with the commands of the gospel in our day.

101

Christian Witness

A third manner in which the laity acts as the Church in the world is through its witness to its faith. Some might insist that this should have been placed first, though the logical sequence seems to me to be as we have discussed the three. Who one is—the Christian exercising his call—is fundamental to what one does—the Christian acting to alleviate human need. And both are basic to the witness of the Christian. Indeed, properly speaking, the first two are part of the layman's witness. He cannot speak an effective word of witness except as it grows out of who he is and what he does.

The preacher-evangelist who insists on segregation is not likely to be effective in working with the Negro, and the layman who goes forth from a local congregation which fails to actualize the fellowship of the Spirit will be less effective in his witness to the world. Yet these other forms of witness are incomplete without the word of witness to the gospel of Jesus Christ; and whatever else is included in the mission of the Church, it is fundamentally to proclaim the reconciling love of God as made known in Jesus Christ.

There are three major forms of Christian witness to which we may give brief attention. There is first the witness of the corporate life of the local congregation. The proclamation of the gospel in liturgy and sermon, in sacrament and teaching, in deed and action—work which involves the corporate Church—is at the heart of the Church's witness. Much of this is the responsibility of the set-apart ministry, and we can take heart in the fact that churches are now more concerned with their life of worship and sacrament and that we are enjoying a renewal of biblical preaching. Although this witness has been broadened within recent years by the use of the mass media (radio, television, the printed word, the motion picture), generally speaking, these forms of proclamation require that the person involved make some move in the direction of the Church, even if nothing more than attending to what is seen on the television screen.

Other forms of the life of the Church, such as its teaching ministry and its group life, for which both laymen and clergy are responsible, also require some movement of the person to the congregation. The effectiveness of teaching groups as a means of evangelism is generally accepted—provided, of course, the unchurched person can be brought into the group. For this to occur laymen must often bring persons into their groups.

The total life of the congregation also is a potential means of witness, though with the divisions within the total body (denominations) and with the lack of real community which often exists in local congregations, part of the effectiveness is lost. Although we can never be satisfied with what now is, we can at least rejoice in what measure of community does exist and can expect its potentiality as a means of proclaiming the gospel to be increased as the inner koinonia is made real by the reception of the Spirit.

A second means of proclamation is through the organized outreach of the Church—the various means by which its mission is given structure in the world. That which we have traditionally called "missions" (a misnomer—it is actually the Church in mission of which we speak) is an example. Without evaluating the effectiveness either in the past or in the present of the Church's organized mission in the world, we must acknowledge that the areas where it may be carried on are rapidly diminishing. In some places the coming of Communism has put a stop to such organized work. In others, where foreign domination has been thrown off and a new nation has arisen (as in India and the African states), there is a suspicion that such organized efforts are too much tainted with imperialism. Increasingly the churches are coming to realize that the nineteenth-century missionary structures, in which a preacher, a teacher, a social worker, or a technical worker was sent under the auspices of a foreign missions board, is probably eventually coming to an end. While the possibilities still remain, we shall of course continue these procedures (as they are, indeed, being expanded in some areas). It is probable, however, that in the future it will be much more common for the work of witness in other lands to be carried on by the lay Christian who goes to that country to carry on his daily work, the work of witness then being done without benefit of formal structure.

The organized work of evangelism in the United States, especially visitation evangelism by laymen, is a similarly structured enterprise. The significance of this type of outreach must not be underestimated. It has been a far cry from the church of my childhood where a two weeks' "revival meeting" in the summer was the extent of organized evangelism. Yet it has become increasingly clear that this might more properly be called "membership enlistment," since most of those visited are already church members or at least nominal Christians. Further, they are normally those who have in one way or another indicated an interest in the congregation—by joining a church-school class, signing a "prospect card" at a worship service, or otherwise indicating their interest. In an age of great population mobility some such form of membership enlistment is essential, but it is hardly adequate as the Church's sole attempt to reach out beyond its corporate life.

One pastor I know has developed in his congregation a small, committed group whose aim is to carry on a deeper kind of evangelism. In their group meetings they are provided with the help they need both in understanding and in knowing how to talk about their faith. Before a visit is made, they must find some opportunity to witness verbally to a group concerning their faith, and often they are asked to make a statement of their faith in writing. The approach they use in their visits is not one which centers in a discussion of church membership but rather in what it means to be a committed Christian.

Partly as the result of the work of these "lay witnesses," as they are called, this congregation has increased its membership considerably, many of those coming into its fellowship never having been members of a church.

The hospital and institutional chaplaincy in another structure which has evolved in our period. The use of the mass media of communication cannot be ignored even in a brief survey. None of these organized structures is likely to prove adequate, however, if the Church's witness is to be made to those completely outside its orbit.

The Lay Apostolate

Therefore we must turn to a third type of witness, that which takes place without benefit of organized structures. We have indicated that in many places and for many people the clergy are suspect. The efforts to break down this dividing wall are all to the good, but the fact remains that this type of witness is supremely the work of the lay apostolate. It is the laity who actually live and work with the unchurched, and it is they through whom the witness must usually occur if it is to occur at all. Nor is it likely to happen unless there is a sound basis in the relationship that one person has established with another, a relationship in which there is mutuality, trust, and confidence.

Frustrating as it may appear to many laymen, there simply are no prearranged structures in which they can operate to make this witness. Arnold Come is no doubt right when he insists "that this kind of Christian witness (martyria) has no predictable, pre-established forms." [26] The lay apostolate must, to a great extent, be on its own even as it was in the first centuries of the Christian movement. No one provided a turnover chart for training the lay witness in those days, and we may be reaching the point where such crutches will be less and less effective today.

105

A few examples may serve to illustrate the wide variety of forms which the lay apostolate may take.

The Christian writer may do it through his writing, even though it may be basically secular in character. Kraemer points to C. S. Lewis as a layman who has made an obvious verbal witness both through speaking and through writing, and to C. E. M. Joad, the philosopher, as one whose witness is more subtle.[27] Many would insist that even the non-Christian writer, such as Albert Camus and Tennessee Williams, by pointing to reality and describing the human predicament, is making a substantial contribution to the Christian witness. The artist can make his witness through his painting, though often when he seeks to paint a "religious" painting, he only copies other Christian paintings.[28]

I know at least two doctors who consider their work to be more than physical healing, using the crisis of illness as a time to discuss with the patient his deeper personal problems. There are psychiatrists who deal with their patients on the religious level, keeping the patient's own faith in mind.[29] Marriage counselors may help their clients find adequate religious faith.[30] In spite of the separation of church and state in the United States, teachers may at times be able to direct their students to their own church for help. One teacher recently expressed her perplexity to me because a pupil had said to her, "I'd like to go to your church." Those who knew her added that the witness of her Christian life was such that it was not uncommon for her students to be attracted to the Christian faith.

The housewife finds her major direction of witness to her children, but she may also find opportunities to discuss the deeper issues of life with her neighbor. By showing genuine concern and entering into the life of another, the manual laborer may be able to witness to his partner in work, the personnel director to his employees, the store manager to his clerks, the lawyer to his clients, the scientist to his colleagues.

The point of contact may be a crisis situation, the everyday problems which sometimes weigh heavily, or the common concerns of the two persons involved. We can use discretion, good taste, even restraint, and yet find the opportunity, if we are secure enough about our faith, to speak the effective word of witness at the proper time.

More structured forms of life, such as the regular meeting of the occupational or professional group, may serve as an opportunity for the consideration of issues in the light of religious faith. This is the pattern sometimes followed by the European lay centers, and the experiments are now being made in the United States in this direction. Such groups are often surprisingly open to Christian comments when they are made within the context of genuine concern. We need to explore what new forms are possible if we are to proclaim the gospel effectively in our post-Christian civilization, for the Church can no longer depend on persons' coming to it. It must increasingly emphasize the necessity of the laity's going to the people. Then and only then will it be expressing its mission and ministry under the command of Christ.

What, then, is the responsibility of the clergy in this enterprise? It is essentially to be the instructor of the evangelist, not so much with respect to method as the content of the Christian faith. "The trained theologian, the pastor and missionary, instead of being regarded as *the* evangelist of the Church—a job for which he is in a particularly bad position—will then be the biblical and theological instructor of the evangelists, a job for which he is in a particularly good position." [31] "Laymen are on the frontline, served by the ministry whose function is to equip the people of God for its mission." [32]

"One of the greatest tasks of the Church today is to grasp clearly the significance of the lay ministry *in* the world." [33]

In these and other statements the volume prepared for the Evanston Assembly of the World Council of Churches spoke with respect to the dual function of clergy and laity in this work of witness. The lay apostolate itself must do much of the actual witnessing, and the role of the clergy is to prepare the lay apostolate for its work in the world.

The question of how the laity is to be prepared for this work remains to be considered, and it is to this that we direct our attention in subsequent chapters.

NOTES

1. Congar, *op. cit.*, pp. 373, 374.
2. *Ibid.*, p. 375, italics his. See also Abbé Michonneau, *Revolution in a City Parish* (London: Blackfriars Publications, 1957), especially pp. 103-7.
3. Kraemer, *op. cit.*, p. 170
4. Arnold B. Come, *op. cit.*, p. 157.
5. See, for example, the article by P. Ricoeur, "Ye Are the Salt of the Earth," in *A Symposium on the Laity, op. cit.*, 39-51.
6. Cf. Franklin H. Littell, *The German Phoenix: Men and Movements in the Church in Germany* (Garden City, N. Y.: Doubleday & Company, Inc., 1960), especially pp. 122-31; and Margaret Frakes, *Bridges to Understanding: The "Academy Movement" in Europe and North America* (Philadelphia: Muhlenberg Press, 1960), *passim*.
7. This was made clear to me in various ways in a summer spent in participating in, observing, and talking with the leaders of the "lay movement" in Europe.
8. August B. Hollinghead, *Elmstown's Youth: The Impact of Social Class on Adolescents* (New York: John Wiley & Sons, Inc., 1949), Chap. 10.
9. This is the title which Robert A. Raines gives to his book, *New Life in the Church* (New York: Harper & Brothers, 1961).
10. Cf. G. Abbott-Smith, *A Manual Greek Lexicon of the New Testament, op. cit.*, p. 249.
11. Paul S. Minear, "Work and Vocation in Scripture," in *Work and Vocation: A Christian Discussion*, ed. John Oliver Nelson (New York: Harper & Brothers, 1954), p. 71.
12. Cf. W. R. Forrester, *Christian Vocation: Studies in Faith and Work* (London: Lutterworth Press, 1951), pp. 33-35.
13. Gustaf Wingren, *Luther on Vocation*, trans. Carl C. Rasmussen (Philadelphia: Muhlenberg Press, 1957), p. 5 and *passim*.
14. Niebuhr, Williams, and Gustafson, *op. cit.*, pp. 64-65.
15. This is the view maintained by Alan Richardson, *The Biblical Doctrine of Work* (Ecumenical Studies No. 1; London: Student Christian Movement Press, 1952), p. 37.
16. Niebuhr, Williams, and Gustafson, *loc. cit.*
17. See James M. Stephens and Edward Leroy Long, Jr., *The Christian as a Doctor* (New York: Association Press, 1960).

18. A series entitled "The Christian in His Vocation," of which the book mentioned in note 17 is an example.
19. A phrase popularized by Vance Packard in *The Hidden Persuaders* (New York: David McKay Co., Inc., 1957).
20. Paul A. Root, now deceased, who taught at Perkins School of Theology, Dallas, Texas, in the 1930's and 1940's.
21. George W. Webber, *God's Colony in Man's World* (Nashville: Abingdon Press, 1960), pp. 93-94.
22. *Ibid.*, p. 94.
23. *Ibid.*, pp. 96-97.
24. *The Church Redemptive, op. cit.*, pp. 133-35.
25. Webber, *op. cit.*, pp. 90-98.
26. Come, *op. cit.*, p. 157.
27. Kraemer, *op. cit.*, p. 115.
28. A fact brought home to me through an exhibit of "religious" paintings at the Tate Gallery, London, in the summer of 1958. The paintings had been commissioned for the exhibit, and by and large showed little originality.
29. See, for example, Paul Tournier, *The Meaning of Persons* (New York: Harper & Brothers, 1957).
30. *Cf.* Hiltner, *op. cit.*, pp. 38-39.
31. "The Laity—The Christian in His Vocation," Part IV of *The Christian Hope and the Task of the Church* (New York: Harper & Brothers, 1954), p. 49. This material is from the Second Assembly of the World Council of Churches held in Evanston, Illinois, in 1954.
32. "Evangelism—The Mission of the Church to Those Outside Her Life," Part II of *ibid.*, p. 59.
33. "The Laity—The Christian in His Vocation," p. 1.

CHAPTER 6

EMERGING PATTERNS OF RENEWAL

In a previous chapter we noted the breakdown of meaning and the experience of estrangement or lostness in the lives of twentieth-century Western man. We have also indicated that at a time when man desperately needs roots, the Church has tended to accommodate itself to a sub-Christian culture, thus denigrating the message of the gospel. We have insisted that the Church can neither ignore its culture nor capitulate to it. Neither liberal theology, which tended to capitulate, nor fundamentalism, which tries to live in a pre-Darwinian world in which modern biblical study is unknown, is adequate as an interpretation of the gospel. What is needed is an approach to the Church's faith which is both true to its essential nature and at the same time relevant to modern man.

I believe we have this in the type of theological thinking which has emerged within recent years. It is the kind of approach which was briefly described in Chapter 2. Resources are available for a new awakening within the worldwide Church.

We can no longer assume that the culture in which we live is Christian, even though it retains many of its Christian qualities. If this is the case, then it means that again, as in the early Christian church, men of faith must live in two worlds. Most of the life of the layman is spent in a sub-Christian, or in Communist countries an anti-Christian, culture. The Church must be *in* but not *of* the world, and so must the individual Christian. The interior life of the Church must make of it a "colony of heaven," but its purpose as a colony is to be an agent of reconciliation to the world. Old patterns of church life are inadequate in preparing the laity for their work both in Church and world. If the social observers are right, then the structures of church life will need to be transformed in order to meet the new needs of our post-Christian culture.

American churches have reacted more positively to the new situation than have those in Europe. The concept of the seven-day-a-week program has been a modern response to the emerging situation, but much of what has evolved is only partially related to the central mission of the Church. Recreation, social affairs, church suppers, scout troops, business meetings, mimeographing, and similar activities, while not necessarily to be avoided, are only partially oriented to the Church's command to preach, teach, and baptize (Matt. 28:19). Neither the pre-twentieth-century structures to which Europe has clung nor the twentieth-century ones which America has developed may be adequate as we enter the new age of space and time.

The Shape of the Pattern

The traditional Protestant descriptions of the Church list only two "marks": preaching and the administration of the sacraments. The Reformed tradition generally adds a third, the maintaining of discipline, or the ordered life. The New Testament is broader in its description, as when, for example, in Acts 2:42 converts are described as devoting themselves "to the apostles' teaching and fellowship, to the breaking of bread and the prayers."

In this analysis I simply assume that corporate worship and preaching and the celebration of the sacraments will be continued. I am concerned with new patterns and structures which supplement the traditional work of the church and will perhaps ultimately replace some of the "activities" which have grown up in the modern American institutional church.

Four needs must be met by these emerging patterns. First, there is the need for a personal group in which the individual can have mediated to him personal identity, mature selfhood, and the reconciling love of God. People caught up in the contingencies of modern culture must have their lives redirected by participation with others in the common Body of Christ, and this has to happen in face-to-face relationships.

Second, there is the need for help in understanding the nature of the faith which is given. "Religion-in-general" will not suffice; nothing short of the biblical faith, rephrased in modern terms, is adequate. This is the process which Rudolf Bultmann calls "demythologizing," and though the term seems to me to be a stumbling block which is just as well avoided, his basic premise is sound: namely, that the truth of the gospel, which is eternal, must be separated from the scientific, intellectual, and emotional forms in which it was stated for other ages, and made relevant and meaningful to our own.

Third, there is the need for that which provides the impetus for action in Church and society. Neither "experiencing the truth" nor "knowing the truth" is adequate alone or together. A third step is necessary, "doing the truth." [1] The layman needs not only the stimulus to act but also help in *how* to act—not blueprints, but the aid which comes from the sharing of both success and failure in the work of vocation, service, and mission, both in Church and world.

Finally, the layman needs the continuing support of a fellowship group as he seeks to know and to do. To some extent this comes through worship and sacrament, but they are not enough. Here too the face-to-face relationships to which we have continually referred are a prime necessity.[2]

112

In other words there is the need for a group in which reconciliation comes alive through the redemptive fellowship, one in which serious study is done, one in which ways and procedures of acting are considered, and one which offers support in the battle of life. It may be the same group which does all four things, or it may be several. The composition of such a group may be constant, or it may vary. Smaller congregations as a whole may perform many of these functions. Existing church groups (church school classes, committees, and the like) may serve the purpose for some and not for others. The family and groups outside the recognized church structure must also be taken into account.

For children, indeed, the family must perform most of the functions of the primary face-to-face group. If the family has broken down in some strata of society, then either it must be restored or we must find a substitute very much like it. For youth the family is still needed, as it is for adults (in the husband-wife relationship). But the family in isolation is not enough—as perhaps it was in a former day. Thus we must take seriously the type of group life adequate to meet the needs of both youth and adults in our day. Though most of the suggestions in the following pages are aimed toward adults, many of them are applicable to youth also.

European Patterns

It seems fair to say that it took World War II to awaken the European church to the fact that its old structures had largely deteriorated. To be sure the process had begun a century earlier. Church membership in the free churches in England has declined steadily since the 1930's,[3] and participation in the established churches had reached an all-time low by the time of World War II. Estimates throughout Europe range anywhere from 1 to 12 or 14 per cent.[4] "Of course we are Christians," a Briton said recently. "But the church is outmoded and dead." [5]

Perhaps the most fruitful movement in the late nineteenth and early twentieth centuries was the Student Christian Movement, along with the World Student Christian Federation. A substantial number of the leaders in both the ecumenical movement and the European church revival were active in the SCM in the period between the two wars. Indeed it was out of this group that the first of the modern conference centers, Sigtuna in Sweden, arose. Initiated as a "People's College" and a center for the "Young Church Movement" in 1917, it began in the 1920's to add short term courses similar to those held by the conference centers today.[6] Iona Community, a group of clergy and laity in the Church of Scotland concerned with church renewal and the rebuilding of Iona Abbey, was initiated by George MacLeod in 1938.[7] CIMADE was begun in France in 1939 as an organization to aid Alsatian refugees, and the idea for and the preliminary work for Taizé had its inception during the war, though the first community was not established until 1945. All the other centers of renewal follow World War II.

It was the impact of the war that awakened small groups of both clergy and laity to the seriousness of the situation. Particularly in the church struggle in Germany under Nazism was there born a new spirit which saw both the need for reform and for relating the Church to the world. The Barmen Declaration of May, 1934, in which some 140 delegates from nineteen territorial churches in Germany declared their uncompromising opposition in the name of Jesus Christ to the Nazi attempt to control the German churches,[8] was a turning point in the struggle. The ringing challenge of this defiance of Hitler is summarized in one sentence: "We repudiate the false teaching that there are areas of our life in which we belong not to Jesus Christ but another lord, areas in which

114

we do not need justification and sanctification through him." [9] Together with the Stuttgart Declaration of Guilt of 1945,[10] this is undoubtedly one of the most significant declarations of faith which has come out of this century, even though comparatively unknown to American Christians.

Out of the travail of persecution, war, occupation, and the other evils which have befallen Europe since the 1930's there has grown a new spirit and there have emerged new forms of church life which are quietly working a reformation in the European church. A new chapter in church history has been and is being written, too little known or acknowledged by the American church. And if the recently published *A Christian in East Germany* is at all typical,[11] the chapter is being continued under Communist domination in the East.

The spirit is more important than the forms which have emerged, and yet one way of understanding the renewal itself is to look at its manifestations. Therefore we shall look briefly at five signs of renewal which have emerged in this movement.

The Conference Center. Perhaps the best known of these efforts is the conference center, or "lay academy" (*Evangelische Akademie* or "church academy") being the name given to the seventeen which have arisen in Germany (fourteen in West Germany, three in East Germany) since 1945. The two earliest were Bad Boll, near Stuttgart, Germany, and Heimstatte Boldern, near Zurich, in Switzerland. More than forty such centers now exist in Finland, France, Germany, Great Britain, Italy, The Netherlands, Sweden, and Switzerland.[12] In addition to those more closely related to national churches there are several completely international, the best known being the Ecumenical Institute at Château de Bossey, near Geneva, Switzerland, under the auspices of the World Council of Churches.

The centers vary so much that it is impossible to describe them in detail in this brief chapter. Further information is available to those who are interested in several recent publications.[13] CIMADE, in Paris, was begun for refugees and still operates in this area, but since World War II has regularly held conferences sometimes with leadership and participation from Roman, Orthodox, and Protestant communions.[14] The Y.M.C.A. "colleges" in England and Wales operate partly as cultural education centers, partly for distinctly Christian purposes. Iona Community is a permanent community of clergy and laity concerned with being an agency of renewal in the Church of Scotland. Its retreat center is located in Iona Abbey on the tiny island of Iona off the Scottish coast. (Here St. Columba came in the sixth century to bring Christianity from Ireland to what is now Scotland.) Conferences are held at the abbey for both members and guests. Agape, a youth camp in the Italian Alps, is under the auspices of the native Waldensian Protestant Church but ecumenical in character. It holds youth camps somewhat on the pattern of American youth conferences. Taizé, for men, and Grandchamps, for women, in Southern France, are communities of permanent members, principally of the Reformed tradition, who are active in the world and especially concerned for the cause of Christian unity. Retreats are also held for visitors, and within recent years colloquies have been held at Taizé for Protestants and Roman Catholics together.

The most common pattern, however, is that followed by the German academies and by similar centers in France, Switzerland, The Netherlands, Sweden, Finland, and England. The emphasis is on the brief conference organized around a theme, or the vocational interest of the participants. It is the hope always that these common interests will be seen in the light of the Christian faith, but no pressure is brought upon those who attend to do so. Worship is held daily, but is voluntary. Bible study is common.

Attendants are not necessarily church leaders, or even active church members. The more common way of securing participants is outside the church structure, through industry, a non-church organization, a labor union. As one observer is quoted as putting it, through them "the church has rediscovered the world, and the world has rediscovered the church." [15] The dialogue between church and world, so long neglected in many European churches, has been re-established in an effective manner through the work of the centers.

The goal in Germany has been for each territorial church to have its own academy. They have developed special interests, partly determined by their leadership and partly by their location. Bad Boll, near the industrial city of Stuttgart, for example, has specialized in conferences for labor and management, while Tutzing, in Bavaria, the artistic center of Germany, has placed special emphasis on work with artists and philosophers. The centers throughout Europe are joined together by an informal association, the purpose of which is to keep the leadership in communication with one another. The Department of the Laity of the World Council of Churches also maintains a friendly relationship with the centers.

One of the major thrusts of the movement has been to gather together persons from the same occupation or profession to consider the relevance of the Christian faith to their work. To indicate the wide variety of focuses which only one of the centers had during a single year, the list for 1957 from Boldern is illuminating. There were several groups for labor plus groups for agricultural engineers, college teachers, bakers, farmers, businesswomen, divorcees, mothers, lawyers, secretaries, salesmen, widows, engaged couples, farmers' servants ("hired hands"), and psychiatrists. During 1958 seventeen German academies held 810 seminars with 43,089 persons participating, on subjects ranging from "The Political Integration of Western Europe" to "The Picture of Man in the Comic Strips" to "The Woman in a Man's World." [16] No one is excluded, one of the centers in Germany spending time working with dancing instructors, who, in middle-class families, exercise considerable influence on teen-agers.[17]

117

My own impression, based on visits to the centers lasting from a few hours to one week, corroborates a common opinion that they are being used as instruments of renewal within the European churches which may result in a deep-rooted if not a spectacular revival. They are above all places where "full and free discussion" on any and all topics may be carried on. Much that they do is unconventional even by American standards. In countries where the Church has had little to do with the common life they are revolutionary. Not every one approves, but many who have questions realize that the situation is sufficiently desperate that only the untried is likely to be effective. They vary in their attempts to maintain contact with the existing church structures. The leader of one center, which has a better relationship with its parent church than some of the others, made it clear that they could never be a tool of the ongoing church. They must stay out ahead of the organized church if they are to serve their proper function, he insisted. Eberhard Müller, who more than any other one man is responsible for their development, has said: "The maintenance of freedom today, and indeed the continued existence of humanity, demands more than ever the ministry of the Church. To pioneer and develop this ministry is the fundamental aim of the Protestant Academies." [18]

Most of what one reads about the centers tends to be overly idealized. The picture that has been painted of the organized church has perhaps been too bleak, whereas that of the lay centers has been on the opposite extreme. Experiences with some of the leaders in the summer of 1961 were reassuring, however, since they indicated that the early, somewhat uncritical appraisal of their work is giving way to a more sober look at the weaknesses and the needs for the future. There is a growing recognition, for example, that the social situation, which has changed from the ravages of war to general prosperity, necessitates somewhat different approaches. These comments are not intended to deny the significance of the movement, however, and there is good reason to believe that they will continue as instruments of renewal of the Church provided they do not become simply another organized movement living off its past achievements.

The Lay Rally. In America, where the "rally" (or large meeting of laymen) is a common occurrence, it may seem odd to include the lay rally in Europe as a sign of renewal. Alone they would not be conclusive; but seen alongside the smaller meetings which have been described, they assume greater significance. One might not inappropriately compare the German *Kirchentag* ("church day") with the camp meeting on the American frontier—both have served as a rallying point for and special emphasis on the Church and its message.

As Eberhard Müller is the leading figure in the Germany academy movement, Reinold von Thadden, a layman, is the guiding figure behind the *Kirchentag.* Like many of the leaders in the lay revival, Von Thadden was active in the Student Christian Movement prior to World War II. Serving as an unwilling officer in the German army during World War II, Von Thadden was captured by the Russians and shipped to a slave-labor camp. It was there, in association with Christians from such backgrounds as Roman Catholicism and the Mennonite community, that the image of the *Kirchentag* was born.[19]

The first of the rallies was held in Hanover in 1949, and hence yearly until 1956, when they were put on a biennial basis. One was held in East Germany, at Leipzig, with ten thousand attending from West Germany and with a total gathering at the closing rally estimated at 650,000. Bible study, addresses, sermons, music and drama programs, and discussions compose the program, which lasts for several days. The most recent of the rallies, held in West Berlin, had fewer in attendance, with some 100,000 at the closing rally. It was in some ways one of the more significant, for the East Germans, forbidden at the last moment both to hold meetings in East

Berlin and to attend the sessions in West Berlin, came in significant numbers. There was also a sizable group from outside Germany, some of whom were brought face to face for the first time with persons who *know* what it is to be Christian, without any question, because of their continual facing of Communist harassment.

Beginning in 1957 a similar rally, known as Kirk Week,[20] has been held in Scotland, and smaller gatherings are held in France and the Netherlands.[21]

The rally alone would be of no great significance, just as the camp meeting in nineteenth-century America was powerless without the continuing nurture of the Christian family. Seen in relation to the small academy movement, however, it takes on greater importance. Further, as a symbol of Christian unity held near, or even within, the Communist orbit and as a rallying point for churchmen, its value should not be underestimated.

The House Church. Another movement, on a lesser scale than the first two, is the House Church movement of England and Scotland, and a similar counterpart in Germany, the industrial cell or *Hauskreis.* The "house church" is an attempt to move the locus of the Church's life partly out of the church building into the homes of members and other interested people. It is an effort to recover the sense of community which constituted the New Testament Church, in terms of people rather than buildings. Different kinds of meetings are held in homes, for groups of a dozen or so people: Bible study, worship, Holy Communion, and the like. Attempts are made to enlist the lapsed, the disinterested, even the unconfirmed in the meetings. Many of the meetings are led by laymen.[22]

A similar kind of meeting is held under the auspices of the academy at Bad Boll, the *Hauskreise,* or "house circles." Held in homes or public buildings, an attempt is made to secure participation by persons completely outside the orbit of the

Church's influence. Similar small group meetings are often held by "alumni" of the academy.

The Industrial Mission. A less-known type of experiment is the industrial mission. Unlike the industrial chaplaincy in the United States (in which a clergyman is employed by industry as a counselor), the industrial mission exists alongside of, not as an integral part of, industry. E. R. (Ted) Wickham carried on such a mission in Sheffield, England, for sixteen years until his recent election to the episcopacy. After work or at tea breaks, both workmen and management gather to discuss issues of concern to them, on the level of what Wickham calls "the secular relevance of the Gospel." [23]

At Mainz-Kastel, Germany, Horst Symanowski has conducted a similar mission, with special emphasis on a resident center for apprentices and theological students.[24] *Haus Villigst* is a social institution in the Ruhr Valley, formerly under the direction of Klaus von Bismark, which conducts seminars for workers and foremen, houses apprentices and engages them in study, and provides a center to which university students may come while they earn money in industry to further their university studies. One of the special projects of *Haus Villigst* has been to preserve and assemble documents regarding Nazism; and, as a history professor on the staff explained, here "we discuss the sorry period thoroughly, as it must be if the same sort of thing is not to happen again." [25] In Berlin, Harald Poelchau has regularly gathered industrial workers together for weekend seminars in a similar effort to evangelize this stratum of German society.

The Part-time Priest. The best known of the efforts to relate the clergy to the world—and thus to the laity—was the worker-priest movement in France and Belgium, now defunct in the former country but, at least until recently, still operating in the latter. The Community House of the Iona Community in Glasgow makes an effort in this direction through giving summer living quarters to theological students who are working during the summer in industry.[26] The lay preacher of Methodism is still alive in England, and in Scotland I met a former Salvation Army lieutenant who had withdrawn from that movement, gone to work in industry, and was in process of beginning a community center to which he hoped to attract industrial workers.

The Church of England is currently exploring the possibilities of a part-time priest movement; that is, the ordination of persons who will continue to be gainfully employed outside the Church to the ministry of word and sacraments, creating an office different from either the lay reader or the perpetual diaconate. F. R. Barry, the Bishop of Southwell, writes as follows in favor of the experiment:

What I am suggesting is a priesthood (equal in authority and commission with that of the whole-time priests whom we know now) which would be exercised and fulfilled partly, or mainly, in "secular" employments, partly in supplementing the whole-time Ministry. (Nobody can be a part-time priest any more than he can be a part-time Christian.) There are not a few men who . . . are unable to accept ordination if that means becoming professional clergymen. They would, however, offer themselves willingly to a supplementary ministry of this kind.[27]

Although the motivation for his suggestion may be primarily to relieve the shortage of clergy, it might well have the effect of increasing the relationship between clergy and laity.

These are all examples of the stirrings of new life within the European churches. Not all of them are lay-centered as such (even the "lay academies" are more often headed by clergymen than by laymen), but all of them affect the Church's conception of the laity. Thus, in one way or another, they all contribute to the concerns which this book reflects; namely, that the Church will rediscover itself as the whole people of God. Further, they indicate that new life is evident within the tired and outworn structures of the European churches. It may be, as many Europeans will argue, that the geographical parish structure is no longer possible in European industrial and urban society. If this is the case then it is possible that out of the ferment which is now evident some new structure will emerge by which the Church will express its life as the twentieth century comes to a close.

American Patterns

We have already seen how American Christianity has been consistently more lay-centered than European. Further, it has been characterized by periodic "revivals," beginning with the first Great Awakening in the mid-eighteenth century and coming on up through Billy Sunday, Dwight L. Moody, and Billy Graham. The frontier camp meeting, the periodic local church "revival meetings" of this century, and the generally higher degree of lay concern have also contributed to the making of American church patterns different from those of Europe. The voluntaryistic principle which has led to an emphasis on "stewardship" (often, unfortunately, associated only with the giving of money) has produced a degree of personal involvement by the laity in church life of which we can be grateful.

But as we have tried to indicate this does not mean that all is well in American church life. Disintegration has already set in in many parts of the nation, and there are those who predict that these same forces will operate throughout America during the second half of the century if something is not done to deepen the life of the churches. Thus our concern must not be just to enlist the disinterested but—perhaps primarily—to disturb the complacent activists who are at work in our churches without sufficient knowledge of what they are about.

The Small Group. To this end the most common pattern thus far developed in the American churches is the small group within the local congregation, for study, fellowship, and action. The adult church-school class has served these purposes in many churches during the last half century, however inadequately it may, at times, have conceived its mission. Prior to that time, the class meeting in Methodism (in England as well as in America, and in the younger churches of other lands) served many of the same functions.[28] Within recent years the small group idea has emerged, at first in student work (where it was often called the "cell," a perfectly good word, which, unfortunately, the Communists have ruined).[29] Since World War II it has caught on among adults, especially for study, and such groups have arisen, often without much effort to organize them, throughout Protestantism.

They follow various patterns, both in character and point of origin. In some instances the full-time clergyman has been responsible for encouraging the formation of many groups within one church. In other instances one or a few groups have been provided by the pastor.[31] In still others laymen, on their own initiative and without clerical leadership, have begun meeting for study and fellowship.[32] In still other cases adult church-school classes have been formed at the Sunday-school hour for such serious study. Other churches have found the Sunday evening hour either before or in place of the evening service a time for deeper study. Such groups sometimes continue over a number of years; others are disbanded at the end of either a specified or indefinite period. They often study the Bible, sometimes a work in theology, at other times a contemporary problem.[33] The variety of form and the spontaneity with which they have arisen give evidence of their vitality and lead one to believe that it is the work of the Spirit in the Church which has led to their widespread growth.

A few specific illustrations will indicate the breadth of both nature and origin. In a large Methodist church in Fort Worth, Texas, a small group of laymen, mostly but not exclusively young couples, initiated under the guidance of the minister of education a church-school class on a depth study basis. Al-

124

though a few numbers were college instructors, others were not even college graduates. The members themselves accepted responsibility for leading the discussion, the first of which was based on Bernhard Anderson's *Toward Understanding the Old Testament*. In a small-town church in East Texas the pastor has regularly conducted a week-night Bible study in which he announces at the beginning of the study that he will introduce into the discussion questions of historical criticism. A pastor of a medium-sized urban church has been able, over some eight years, to involve about half of his membership in an eight months' course in biblical theology.

A Wesley Foundation director in the South has organized informal courses in Bible and theology to which both university students and town people are welcomed as participants, with about an equal number from the two groups being engaged. A group of a dozen or so persons, couples and single adults, regularly met on Sunday evening without formal leadership (the pastor attended as he was able) to discuss together some work on theology which the entire group was reading. A group of young couples spent four months of study together, meeting semiweekly in order to develop themselves as specialists in one unit of study which they could then teach to other groups. In a midwestern church the minister of education served as co-ordinator for a large number of study groups, meeting with the lay leaders regularly much as the preachers were expected to meet with early Methodist class leaders. Some experiments have been conducted in meetings for occupational groups where the problems of and opportunities for acting Christianly in some profession or occupation are seriously considered. To these examples may be added the formal reports of the work of Robert Chiles,[34] Robert Raines,[35] the First Presbyterian Church of Rahway, New Jersey[36] (with the center now moved to Bloomfield College), and those included in John L. Casteel's composite volume.[37]

One further development in the student field may be reported in more detail. When a new team ministry took over the leadership of the Wesley Foundation at the University of Texas in the summer of 1960, they began to work toward a creative expression of concern for the 4,500 Methodist students enrolled in the university. But how could they possibly reach that many students, most of whom never bothered to come to the small building adjacent to the campus which, if any substantial number should come, would be completely inadequate to accommodate them? So a plan for training a group of students to infiltrate the campus and its organizations was conceived, beginning with a small group given special education to fit them for being witnesses to the campus.

In the fall of 1960 thirty students entered the "Guild of Lay Theologians," a program similar to one begun several years previously at the University of North Carolina and since then adopted by several other colleges. A course of study embracing four years has been projected, subject to revision as the plan unfolds. The first year began with a section dealing with modern theologizing, which was followed by one on "The Heretofore Life of the Church" (Bible, church history), and was concluded with a section centered on the contemporary church in its gathered and scattered manifestations. Each of the three small groups met weekly with an assigned reading made available to each, and with collateral reading accessible in the Foundation library. A second class began its study in the fall of 1961, and this is to be repeated yearly so long as the plan continues. It is the expectation that those who participate will see their study not only as an academic exercise but also as preparation for their mission to fellow students of the university, with the final year in particular emphasizing witness. During its first year the president of the freshman class, a sorority president, a participant in a Negro co-operative housing project, and other campus leaders were involved.[38]

Many of these examples are from my own personal knowledge. Were a person from another section of the country and from another communion collating the data, I am convinced that he might have an equally imposing array of material to offer from his own experience.

In spite of impressions I may have given to the contrary, I am convinced that the local church structure in American Protestantism can be revived. My optimism does not lie in what I see now being done by the average congregation but rather in what I see the Holy Spirit doing among both the laity and the clergy. The future can be hopeful if we open our minds and hearts to his leading.

The Lay Center. Just as the small group is not new in American Protestantism, neither is the lay training center away from the local parish without precedent. The camp meeting is perhaps the prototype of later manifestations. The first such center was established as a result of a conference for Sunday-school workers held in 1874 at Lake Chautauqua, New York, under the leadership of John H. Vincent and Lewis Miller. Chautauqua soon outgrew its exclusive preoccupation with training Sunday-school workers and became a cultural as well as a Christian adult education center. Other centers were soon established.

The early twentieth century witnessed the origin of the summer conference for young people; and the youth camp, conference, and institute became, from the 1930's on, probably the most significant phase of youth work in the Church. As one who can trace part of his active concern for the Christian cause to such conferences, I cannot help resenting a bit those who see in the emergence of the conference center in our day something entirely new. In the period just before and since World War II more and more denominations and local churches have built their own camp and conference centers and have found that they provide facilities not only for young people but also for adults.

To be sure most of the emphasis for adults has been placed

127

on training special leadership, such as church-school workers, leaders of committees on missions, and the like. This has not been true for young people, however; and young adults after World War II came increasingly to hold weekend retreats on a broader basis than leadership training. Within more recent years more mature adults have also entered into serious study at such centers.[39]

More than a quarter of a century ago the Quakers established Pendle Hill at Wallingford, Pennsylvania, as a year-round study center, "bringing to meditation and study the Christians of many denominations and also many foreign students of differing faiths during their stay in the United States." [40] Kirkridge, near Bangor, Pennsylvania, was established for similar purposes in 1941.[41] A residential center was established by the Episcopal Church in 1948 at Parishfield, Brighton, Michigan, but is open to all denominations. "Lay people attending week-end meetings are brought into the daily discipline of the community, sharing worship, study, physical work and recreation with the permanent residents." [42] The United Church of Canada has established four lay training centers: the Prairie Christian Training Center, at Fort Qu'Appelle, Saskatchewan; the Five Oaks Christian Workers Center, at Paris, Ontario; the Atlantic Christian Training Center, at Tatamogouche, Nova Scotia; and the Christian Leadership Training School, at Naramata, British Columbia.[43]

In 1952 a unique experiment was launched in Austin, Texas, as a resident community for students at the University of Texas. Providing dormitory facilities for students (now normally restricted to one year), it also makes available noncredit classes in the meaning of the Christian faith. Its purposes are to seek "new understandings of the Church," "new structures for the Church," "new procedures for the Church," and "new disciplines for the Church" "as mission in the new world." [44] In 1959 a new phase of the venture was launched, the "Laos House," where short courses are offered for both clergy and laity from local congregations, "to meet the needs of an increasing number of persons both inside and outside the Church who are seeking a theological education adequate to their desire for intellectual honesty and integrity." [45]

The Yokefellow Movement, under the leadership of Elton Trueblood, led, in 1956, to the founding of Yokefellow House in Richmond, Indiana, where two-day and one-week institutes have been held since that time. Neither the movement nor the house desires to draw people away from the Church but rather it is "a reformation within the church that brings to the nominal member a new commitment and understanding of his participation in the Christian Community." [46]

So numerous have these centers and experiments become that Margaret Frakes lists twenty-two, of a varied character;[47] and her list does not include, among others, the work of the United Lutheran Church,[48] the center established at Fern Mountain, near Muskogee, Oklahoma, by the Diocese of Oklahoma of the Protestant Episcopal Church, and others which Franklin Littell lists in his account.[49] Nor is it possible to begin to note all the efforts of a less permanent nature held at various denominational camp and conference sites, or even in local churches along the pattern recently evolved by a group of Methodist ministers in San Antonio, Texas, and called a "lay academy." [50]

Parish Life Renewal. To some extent all the efforts toward establishing study groups within local parishes are examples of "parish life renewal." Further there are efforts such as the "Parish Life Program" of the Episcopal Church, which sponsors "parish weekends" for small groups of churchmen during which they consider the nature and mission of the Church as well as their particular responsibilities.[51]

There are examples of more radical forms of parish renewal, the best known of which is the East Harlem Protestant Parish, with its "store-front churches," its group ministry, and its efforts to deal with slum dwellers in terms of their basic

129

human needs.[52] Similar parishes have been established in Chicago and Cleveland by members of the original team ministry. The Church of the Savior in Washington, D.C., is a further example of an attempt to deal with the rejected, the dissident, and the dissatisfied from higher strata of society.[53] The Judson Memorial Church in New York City, begun in 1948, is another example of such experimentation.[54] Imaginative work has also been done by members of the Inner City Mission in the inner city churches of Chicago. In rural areas the larger parish plan, consisting of several churches joined together under a group or team ministry, has been found quite useful but has not been developed as extensively as the situation demands.[55]

Unfortunately the examples of creative parish renewal are not as common as one could wish. Gibson Winter has concluded that Protestant churches are generally introverted; that is, so concerned with their own lives that they are not especially interested in the larger problems of community and world.[56] This has come about, he believes, because of the privatization of the religious sphere, or the confining of religious concerns to personal matters—the maintaining of "the emotional balance of the membership, the nurture of children, and the preservation of a harmonious residential milieu." [57] As a consequence the churches are not especially concerned with whether they serve the community except as that service helps them maintain their own status.

To remedy these conditions he proposes radical changes in congregational life which would touch such areas as the inner city—that is, those parts of a city where previously the middle class has lived but which have now become slums or near slums. Such communities, he believes, should be included in a cross-section area of a metropolis, the larger area involving all types of communities and all classes and having a total strategy worked out by all congregations in the area together. This would mean that clergy and laity together would be concerned not only with their own congregation but also with all others in the sector.[58]

Whether this particular plan is workable is not our task to assess. It does remind us of the possibilities which exist when an imaginative approach to congregational life is taken. Indeed as we face the problems that increased urbanization and secularization will undoubtedly intensify, it may be necessary for us to search for new forms of church life which are not necessarily centered in a building. It may be necessary for us to move into apartments, factories, office buildings, and other places where people carry on their daily lives if we are to make the Church real in our world. We must be willing to cast aside old structures—or at least to supplement them—if the churches are to be truly the Church in the twentieth century.

In spite of this less hopeful note concerning parish renewal, there is much to give us hope in the current situation in the Church. The task ahead is one which calls for both zeal and enlightenment, will and understanding. Thus the aim of the concerns which we shall consider in the following chapters is not simply that laymen will be informed but also that they will be motivated to act as living ministers of Christ, ambassadors in all stations in life of the reconciling love of God.

NOTES

1. From the title of the book by James A. Pike, *Doing the Truth; A Summary of Christian Ethics* (Garden City, N. Y.: Doubleday & Company, Inc., 1955.)
2. These four may be compared with those of Douglas P. Blatherwick: "The Layman Must Know"; "The Layman Must Care"; "The Layman Must Live His Faith"; and "The Layman Must Fall Without the Inner Fellowship," in *A Layman Speaks,* op. cit., Chaps. 5-8.
3. *Ibid.,* p. 104. Blatherwick's figures about the number who at least occasionally attend church services are more optimistic than most. In any case the decrease over the years is obvious, especially in industrial areas. See p. 103.
4. Cf. Margaret Frakes' analysis of the situation in *Bridges to Understanding:*

The "*Academy Movement*" in Europe and North America, op. cit., pp. 1-9.
5. *Ibid.*, p. 2.
6. *Signs of Renewal: The Life of the Lay Institute in Europe*, ed. Hans-Ruedi Weber (Geneva: World Council of Churches, 17, Route de Malagnou, 1956, 1957), pp. 12-13; Frakes, op. cit., pp. 10 ff.
7. This story was told originally by George MacLeod, *We Shall Re-Build: The Work of Iona Community on Mainland and on Island* (Glasgow: The Iona Community, n.d.).
8. Littell, op. cit., Chaps. 1 and 3.
9. *Ibid.*, p. 186; the entire text is found on pp. 184-88.
10. *Ibid.*, pp. 189-90 for the text.
11. Johannes Hamel, *A Christian in East Germany*, trans. Ruth and Charles C. West (New York: Association Press, 1960). Those who say there are no Christians under Communism should read these chapters.
12. Several listings are available: in Weber, *Signs of Renewal*, pp. 61-63; in Littell, op. cit., 202-10; and in Frakes, op. cit., pp. 125-28. The Department of the Laity of the World Council of Churches also maintains listings of the centers.
13. In Weber, *Signs of Renewal*; Littell, op. cit.; and Frakes, op. cit. See also the leaflet, "The Awakening of the Laity in Europe," available from the World Council of Churches. Part of my information also comes from personal visits to the centers made in the summer of 1958.
14. According to information furnished me by the secretary, Jacques Beaumont, in 1958.
15. Frakes, op. cit., p. 66.
16. For a list of the topics, see Littell, op. cit., pp. 127-30; see also *A New Road in Germany: Evangelical Academy*, ed. Martin Koller (Furche-Verlag Hamburg 30, or Evangelische Akademie Württemberg, Bad Boll über Göppingen, Württemberg, Germany), pp. 38-44.
17. Littell, op cit., pp. 131-3.
18. Eberhard Müller, "The Protestant Academies in Germany," in *Signs of Renewal*, p. 11.
19. Littell, op. cit., pp. 79-85.
20. *Ibid.*, p. 103.
21. Frakes, op. cit., pp. 93-96.
22. A full account of this movement is found in E. W. Southcott, *The Parish Comes Alive* (London: A. R. Mowbray & Co., Limited, 1956). The plan has also been used in Scotland.
23. A brief description of this project is found in Webber, *God's Colony in Man's World*, op. cit., pp. 119-20. Bishop Wickham's analysis of the Sheffield situation is found in *Church and People in an Industrial City* (London: Lutterworth Press, 1957), Chap. 6, especially pp. 232-35, 243-54.
24. Webber, *God's Colony in Man's World*, op. cit., p. 120.
25. Frakes, op. cit., p. 55.
26. T. Ralph Morton, "The Iona Community and the Training of the Laity in Scotland," in *Signs of Renewal*, p. 25.
27. F. R. Barry, "The Case for Part Time Priests," in *Part Time Priests? A Discussion*, ed. Robin Denniston (London: Skeffington, 1960), pp. 14-15.

28. For a recent discussion of various phases of the class meeting, see *Spiritual Renewal for Methodism*, ed. Samuel Emerick (Nashville: Methodist Evangelistic Materials, 1908 Grand Avenue, 1958).
29. For a discussion of this movement, see Harvey Seifert, *Fellowships of Concern: A Manual on the Cell Group Process* (New York and Nashville: Abingdon-Cokesbury Press, 1949).
30. See, for example, Carl R. Smith and Robert W. Lynn, "Experiment in Suburbia," in *Spiritual Renewal Through Personal Groups*, ed. John L. Casteel (New York: Association Press, 1957), Chap. 8.
31. See, for example, Raines, *op. cit.*, especially Chap. 11; also Robert E. Chiles, "Laymen Study Theology," *The Pastor*, XIX (July, 1956), No. 17, p. 30.
32. See, for example, Thomas M. Steen, "Renewal in the Church," in Casteel, *op. cit.*, Chap. 1.
33. The variety of books now available is encouraging, even for those groups which are not willing at the beginning to tackle the more difficult ones in Bible and theology. "Reflection Books," a series published by Association Press, as well as their Haddam House books, and "The Layman's Theological Library," published by The Westminster Press, are two series in which a number of useful titles are available. Denominations are also making books available, such as "The Church's Teaching" of the Protestant Episcopal Church and the "Basic Christian Books" of The Methodist Church. With the widespread availability of theological classics now in paperbacks, the supply is almost limitless.
34. Chiles, *op. cit.*
35. Raines, *op. cit.*
36. Frakes, *op. cit.*, p. 103; also pp. 103-6 for other illustrations.
37. Casteel, *op. cit.*
38. Information may be secured from the Rev. Robert Breihan, The Wesley Foundation, 2434 Guadalupe, Austin 5, Texas. His associates were the Rev. L. E. Philbrook and the Rev. Edwin Shaw.
39. For example, the Texas Conference of The Methodist Church, under the direction of the Rev. Richard T. Murray, held a number of such conferences at its assembly grounds, Lakeview, near Palestine, Texas, in 1958-61.
40. "Laity Trends in North America," published by the World Council of Churches as part of its "Laity Packet."
41. Frakes, *op. cit.*, pp. 119-20.
42. "Laity Trends in North America."
43. *Ibid.*; Littell, *op. cit.*, p. 159.
44. From a brochure published by the Christian Faith and Life Community "Break Through." Further information may be secured from the director, the Rev. W. Jack Lewis, 2503 Rio Grande, Austin, Texas.
45. From a leaflet published by the Community, "The Laic Theological Studies," further information being available at the address listed above.
46. From a leaflet published by the Yokefellow House. Further information may be secured by writing to the director, Samuel Emerick, 228 College Avenue, Richmond, Indiana.
47. Frakes, *op. cit.*, pp. 128-29.
48. Littell, *op. cit.*, pp. 159-60.

49. *Ibid.*, p. 158; see also pp. 157-65.
50. The first series of classes is described in a brochure, "Lay Academy." They were conducted each Monday evening beginning February 13, 1961, and continuing through May 1. The Rev. Claus H. Rohlfs is listed as the acting dean, and Mr. Leonard E. Davis, acting registrar, 1101 Frost Bank Building, San Antonio 5, Texas. Another series was begun in the autumn.
51. Frakes, *op. cit.*, pp. 111-12; see also the manual for guidance in the program, *A Parish Workshop in Christian Education* ed. Donald W. Crawford (Greenwich, Conn.: The Seabury Press, 1953).
52. Webber, *God's Colony in Man's World, op. cit.*, especially Introduction.
53. William T. Ham, "Candles of the Lord," in Casteel, *op. cit.*, Chap. 9.
54. "Laity Trends in North America."
55. A presentation of this plan will be found in Marvin T. Judy, *The Larger Parish and Group Ministry* (Nashville: Abingdon Press, 1959).
56. Winter, *op. cit.*, Chap. 5.
57. *Ibid.*, p. 134; see also pp. 131-40.
58. *Ibid.*, pp. 144-49.

CHAPTER 7

MEANS TOWARD RENEWAL

Although this book is not intended as a manual for small groups or even as a structured plan for involving lay people in the Church, it seems appropriate that brief comments be made with respect to methods for implementing some of the concerns expressed in earlier chapters. Both structures and methods are only means to an end and must evolve, to some extent, out of a particular situation. We have seen in the previous chapter how the renewal of the Church is taking diverse forms and following multiple paths, and this is as it should be. On the other hand we have also noted that similarities in patterns have emerged, often independently. There are, then, certain general suggestions which should be helpful to those interested in the point of view which has been presented, and it is to some of these that we now turn.

Major Emphases

Two of the major emphases in the new forms of church life are fellowship, or koinonia, and study. A third grows out of these two, or in some instances may contribute to them: action, or the doing of the truth. In other terms, there is a concern for participation in the Christian faith community, for it is in this manner that we are drawn meaningfully into the fellowship of faith and receive the gift of God's love and grace

135

through fellowship. But there is a correlative interest, directed toward a deepened *knowledge* of what it means to be a participant, a man of faith, a committed Christian.

Without commitment, knowledge is sterile. A new gnosticism (salvation through right knowledge) is always a threat, and it has reappeared in our day among those who become proud of the fact that they can understand—or at least quote from—Paul Tillich and Reinhold Niebuhr. Participation without knowledge, however, easily becomes a shallow pietism, a subjective romanticism without roots in the Christian tradition, a travesty on the biblical faith. And we have already had enough of *that* in American Protestantism! Both, it may be noted, remain incomplete unless they lead to action in society, in vocation, service, and witness. Both fellowship and knowledge must continually point beyond themselves to the life of action.

Fellowship and learning ought to be closely interrelated, for the group which is concerned only with fellowship—or even praying together—easily succumbs to spiritual snobbery. While the study group is in danger of intellectual snobbery, this is less likely to happen if it has also become a concerned group. Unless the group is turned outward to the lives of others, however, this ingrownness is a constant threat. Of the two emphases as a beginning point (that is, fellowship or study), I am inclined to favor the latter, and thus much of what is included in this chapter pertains to study and learning.

Two separate kinds of help are available in our day for the study-fellowship group. The recovery of theology, especially biblical theology, and the publication of many sound books understandable to the thoughtful layman provide resources for study which were simply not available even a decade ago.[1] Then from a field quite outside the Church, we have been provided with new insights into the nature and functioning of small groups. The knowledge of "group dynamics," a term often improperly used to describe a method, may be utilized to bring about the kind of participation in Church groups which can serve as a medium for koinonia.[2] It is as though in the fullness of time these two factors had been providentially brought into juxtaposition with one another.

At first glance the two may seem to offer opposing points of view. On the one hand, theology has affirmed anew the sovereignty of God, the lordship of Christ, the activity of the Holy Spirit, the falseness of salvation by works-righteousness, the necessity of renewal within the Church. On the other hand there has appeared an approach to method which places emphasis on group study, participation with one another, a non-authoritarian type of teaching, and involvement with one another. On further thought, however, it becomes clear that as a matter of fact they complement each other.

If God is the only ultimate authority, as theologians insist, then man is in need of a maximum amount of help in discovering what is the will of God for him in a particular situation or set of circumstances. No attempt has been made in Protestantism to return either to an authoritarian view of the Church or to a narrow interpretation of the Scriptures. Rather, the emphasis is on a view of the Church which recognizes it as consisting of a concerned, searching people, in which the Holy Spirit becomes real through community. There is also the further recognition that our existential problems are too complex for any simple, direct answer to be found for most of them in a literalistic interpretation of Scripture.

There is, to be sure, the danger of the tyranny of the group, of "groupthink," where the group dictates to the individual. There are those who would use the insights from the group development field as means of controlling the actions of persons. But this is not the approach which is suggested in its adaptation for Church use. Rather, the emphasis is on the guidance and support which the group can offer the individual

137

in the making and implementing of decisions, in the arriving at understandings, and in the search for meaning and reality.

In this search the disciplined and concerned group within the Church, utilizing the insights of the secular social sciences, is an indispensable aid.

Personal Involvement

Involvement is the word which best describes the quality of group life which is most conducive to both learning and *koinonia*. Perhaps it has become too much of a cliché by enthusiasts of group dynamics, and participation or engagement may be used in its place. Whatever word is used, it points to common sharing in the lives and experience of others. It hardly seems improper to assert that it was the involvement of Christians with one another in the early Church which served as a medium for the work of the Spirit. John Wesley recognized the importance of this when, in speaking of the Methodist class meeting, he wrote:

It can scarce be conceived what advantages have been reaped from this little prudential regulation. Many now happily experienced that Christian fellowship of which they had not so much as an idea before. They began to "bear one another's burdens," and naturally to "care for each other." As they had daily a more intimate acquaintance with, so they had a more endeared affection for, each other.[3]

From quite a different perspective a recent writer in adult education has expressed a similar point of view:

Of all the factors pertaining to success in learning, the most critical are those of motivation—how a person deeply engages himself in the learning transaction. Subject matter, environmental factors, methods, and techniques are also important, but they must be seen in the light of the key word engagement.[4]

138

Motivation is often thought of as the effort to find some external means, such as grades, praise or blame, shame, or other forms of manipulation, to induce learning. Whether or not we can be completely free of such exterior motivations is a question with which I have long struggled without receiving a clear answer. There is some truth in the assertion that through such a means a person may be drawn into a situation in which he will later become personally involved. This is the Church's rationale for using different kinds of "bait" to get people into a church setting—recreation, church suppers, attendance awards, contests, and the life. If such methods are used in the Church, we must be fully aware of their weaknesses (that is, not necessarily effective) and their dangers (that is, the exterior reason may become the whole reason for the existence of the church, whereby it will lose its life in its attempt to find it). Unfortunately also, such procedures may get people involved in the means only, not in that to which the means point.

In any case our goal is personal involvement in meaningful experiences of worship, learning, planning, work, fellowship. Through such engagement in a Christian setting it is hoped that real *koinonia* will evolve.

The Role of the Leader

If personal involvement by all members of the group is our concern, then what is the role of the leader? Although some very informal groups may have no designated leaders, this is the exception. Others, whether they be study, fellowship, or planning groups, require some degree of leadership. If the participation of the entire group is to be encouraged, then the purpose of the leader is not to dominate but to guide and encourage group planning and activity.

To state it in other terms, the purpose of the leader is to provide a setting in which the group can operate at its maximum potential. This may include such details as arranging chairs in a circle so that participants may talk to each other, not just to the leader. He should see that needed equipment, such as a chalkboard, is available. He then encourages group participation, maintaining a permissive atmosphere which makes for maximum freedom of expression. At times he may raise questions, remind the group that they have wandered far from the topic in hand, and summarize when appropriate. In a planning group where a decision is needed and consensus is not obvious, he must help the group decide whether to postpone a decision, arrive at a majority decision, or report two opposing points of view.[5]

The leader of a learning-teaching group likewise is responsible, along with other members, for the providing of a setting in which learning may take place; but he also, again with the help of group members, must see that "learning tasks" are made available.[6] (In the case of a formal teaching situation, the teacher alone may be responsible for this.) Learning tasks consist of printed material to be read, a lecture to be listened to, a film to be seen and heard, a question to be discussed, a project to be carried out, and so on. Whether the leadership is constant or shifts from time to time, some person or group must assume the responsibility for at least minimum structuring of the learning situation.

The learning situation thus involves both the persons who are involved and, if it is Christian, the content of the gospel. The purpose of Christian teaching is to move beyond the mere talking *about* the gospel to a personal confrontation with God as revealed in Jesus Christ. This occurs not only because group members are confronted with subject matter but also because they are confronted by one another.

In more structured groups and in more formal teaching situations, the leader or the teacher may take more of an active role,[7] though here too it is hoped that members will become personally involved. Maximum learning is more likely to occur, especially if it involves more than subject matter, when persons become concerned with one another as well as with the materials with which they are confronted.

A Small Group

Much of what was said in previous paragraphs is applicable to both the large and the small group. It is the latter, however, which concerns us most as a new emphasis in the renewal of the Church.

It is not our purpose here to offer technical help in the field of group process[8] but rather to make elementary suggestions which may be utilized by any church leader in his attempts to improve the group life of the Church. Although these suggestions are, I believe, applicable to committees, planning groups, teachers' meetings, and fellowship groups, I am most concerned with their meaning for the study group.

Three guiding principles seem crucial. First, the group must be small enough for personal interaction—or, in other words, it must be a face-to-face group. Twelve may be a maximally productive number, though a group may be smaller and, I believe, as large as twenty or slightly more. Indeed certain qualities of good group life may come into being when there are twenty-five or thirty; and it is our hope that to some extent an entire congregation may realize its potential as a community. Six to eighteen is probably the range of maximum productivity, however, and some would insist on a maximum of seven or eight.

Second, the group must be sufficiently disciplined for order to be maintained. It cannot wander at will, whether it be a planning group or a study group. Maves' distinction between "task centered" and "need centered" groups[9] is a legitimate one, and he is no doubt right when he insists that the Church ought to have more groups which seek specifically to answer men's needs, not engage them in a particular task. But even a group which is quite free to deal with immediate needs must be ordered so as to deal with those needs, and further, a task to which people give themselves may actually become the cohesive element which forms a group and makes it capable of dealing with needs.

Third, the group must be sufficiently structured so as to accomplish its purpose. Some leadership, except in the most informal situation, is necessary, even though it may shift from time to time, even within the same session.

Two examples may illustrate this point. I was asked to meet with an informal study group that claimed to have no leadership at all. Yet it became evident to me that at least for that evening the member who had invited me was a "hidden" leader. He did not dominate but he did serve as a kind of steering person. In another instance in which I was asked to lead a group that already had considerable cohesiveness but where the leadership did in fact shift from time to time, I found myself about midway in the discussion no longer the leader! Since I was, in a manner of speaking, a "guest" of the group, my first reaction was resentment—a very human reaction, I fear!—and some of the group members apparently felt similarly, for they began—probably wrongly—to shift the leadership back to me.

Generally speaking these small, face-to-face groups do not need to be greatly conscious of methodology, except to be sure that no one person dominates and that everyone is encouraged to speak. As we shall see shortly, some method of acquiring material to discuss and some means of launching the discussion are needed.

The Larger Group

Since it is not possible for all groups to be of the size suggested above, church leaders also must be aware of the possibility of achieving some measure of group cohesion in the larger group. Various techniques are available to assist in this process. For example, it is possible to break the larger group into smaller ones (the "buzz" or "huddle" group) for short periods of time. Such a small group (one person with his neighbor, or four to six persons together when chairs are movable) may discuss a question and report back to the larger group (a reporter must be selected for the report), or it may be asked to raise a question or to react, favorably or unfavorably, to what has been said in a presentation, or to serve as a "listening group" for a film presentation, and so on.

A panel, in which three or four persons discuss one or more questions before the entire group, with no prepared speeches, involves at least a few people, and often—according to my experience—elicits response even from the larger group. A symposium, in which two or more people present brief prepared statements, tends to be formal, and is really an alternative to the lecture. The colloquy may be used, with a moderator, a panel of resource persons to respond to questions, and either the entire group or a representative panel from the audience, participating with the panel of resource persons.[10]

Although most of these suggestions are generally associated with the teaching-learning situation, there is no reason why they could not be used in planning and administrative groups. By and large we have made little effort to use methods of group involvement in official groups which are too large for real group discussion. As a consequence those who speak are likely to be the more extroverted ones and not necessarily those whose ideas are most useful.

Let us repeat that each congregation ought to have as many small groups as possible. If they are properly used, each will become something of a "buzz group" within the total congregation. This means, of course, that there must be some method of "feedback" from the small group to the official body of the church. Perhaps there is no solution to the problem of the large congregation except one which involves some sort of structure that makes possible maximum discussion of important issues in face-to-face groups, with a means of feeding the results of such discussion to the official body of the congregation.

Starting Study Groups

Thus far most of what has been said in this chapter may be applied both to existing groups in the church and to new ones which may be started. We shall now turn specifically to the small study group, the development of which has been noted as an increasingly common pattern in the American churches. By this I mean the group of fewer than twenty members who desire to come to grips with the Christian faith and with themselves before God. Generally speaking, we assume that such persons have already been motivated by a sermon, by the increasingly difficult questions asked by their children, by a personal crisis for which they found themselves unprepared, by the challenge which knowledgeable friends of other faiths present, or by some other reason. An invitation by pastor, director of Christian education, or friend—even an announcement in the church bulletin—may be sufficient to elicit interest. There is, in fact, an atmosphere in both culture and church which encourages adults to increase their knowledge, a fact which has resulted in the burgeoning of adult education enterprises within recent decades.[11] Although it is hoped that the groups we are considering will not be directed merely toward acquiring knowledge *about* the Christian faith, the motives which first evoke participation need not be those which develop as the group proceeds.

We have already seen how such groups in practice vary in their point of origin. A pastor may invite a few interested persons to such a group; laymen themselves may join together either with or without the leadership of a member of a church staff; or an existing group (such as a Sunday-school class) may begin to take more seriously its study responsibilities. It is doubtful whether anything other than free and voluntary participation ought to be encouraged; and at the initial meeting of the group it should be made clear that some study outside class is expected.

Since local congregations and denominations vary with respect to their desire to control what happens in the educational life of the church, any group must be aware of and take into account such limitations. Often the committee on education must approve any official or semiofficial group. Normally, I believe, the kind of groups with which we are concerned should be formed with the knowledge of the pastor or director of Christian education, under the auspices of the official education committee. If such approval is withheld, then there is no reason why adults are not free to form themselves in study groups meeting in their homes and outside the structure of the congregation. It should be noted, however, that this is the manner in which many of the "hate" and extreme "right-wing" groups have originated.

Specific illustrations as to how they begin will be found in the literature on the formation of small groups.[12] Three examples here may prove helpful. In one congregation a few adults approached the minister of education with their desire to form a serious study group meeting at the Sunday-school hour. He encouraged them, but the initiative remained with the laymen. Also with his help the group, after it was formed, decided on their study materials and worked out a rotating plan for the sharing of leadership in leading the discussion.

In another instance I was a guest teacher in a church in which we discussed the possibilities of small-group study. After the final session a woman stopped to discuss where she could find a place to engage in such study since she was dissatisfied with her own adult Sunday-school class. I suggested that she begin talking with her friends and then talk with the

145

director of Christian education about such a group. Later I talked with the director, and she agreed to follow up if nothing had occurred within a reasonable period of time.

In still another case a student in a theological school, working as a field-work student in a local church, began a Sunday-morning study group under the auspices of the education committee. He continued his leadership for three years and then passed it on to other theology students, with a continued emphasis on total group study and participation.

The encouraging thing, as we have seen, is that such groups are emerging throughout the nation. Further, they began to emerge without any set plan and often without a particular group's knowing that other groups were engaging in a similar enterprise. The pattern of origin has been similar to that of the study centers in Europe: the idea originated in several different places simultaneously, and as these began to operate still others were encouraged to launch similar experiments.

Types of Study

One further note may be useful with respect to such study groups; namely, the kind of study which is taking place. We shall consider both subject matter and approaches to study and teaching.

Subject Matter. Whatever may be the specific content of the depth study with which we are concerned, its two focuses must be kept to the fore: on the one hand the biblical faith and on the other, the human situation. We are concerned neither with abstract theologizing nor with an uninstructed discussion of existence, but rather with the two in relationship. We may start with a human problem (the "given" of the human situation) and consider it in the light of the gospel; or we may begin with the gospel (the "given" of the biblical faith) and see its relevance to life. In both cases a too-facile kind of juxtaposition of the two is to be avoided; that is, the adaptation of the "proof-text" method of study on a more sophisticated level. Neither the biblical faith nor human existence is so simple as to lead to an uncomplicated and automatic "correlation" of the two, to use Paul Tillich's term, though it is his "method of correlation" which is suggested.[13] By this he means that the Christian gospel provides "answers" —in the broad sense of the word—to the problems of human existence.

Whatever the beginning point, some piece of material must usually be available for the study group. If they refuse to do outside work, there is little hope that significant learning will occur. For example, a beginning group might commence with the Reflection book, *The Unfolding Drama of the Bible* by Bernhard Anderson. A somewhat more advanced group might use his longer book, *The Rediscovery of the Bible* (Association Press), Suzanne de Dietrich's *The Witnessing Community* (The Westminster Press), or C. H. Dodd's *The Bible Today* (Cambridge University Press). All of these books present an overview of the Bible, something which most adults need before they can make much sense out of individual books and chapters. In all these instances additional resource material is needed, such as *The Interpreter's Bible* (Abingdon), a Bible dictionary, such as those published by Westminster and Harpers, a Greek lexicon—if someone knows even a little Greek— and a biblical word study such as that edited by Alan Richardson, *Theological Word Book of the Bible* (Macmillan). As a group progresses in its study, it will want to utilize the writings of scholars such as Rudolf Bultmann, Oscar Cullman, and Karl Barth.

Or it may be that a group will prefer to begin with a subject more directly related to their own lives. One of the Reflection books (Association Press) might be used: Alexander Miller's *Christian Faith and My Job*, J. H. Oldham's *Life Is Commitment*, Stephen Neill's *The Difference in Being a Christian*, or Robert L. Calhoun's *God and the Day's Work*. (There are

147

many other appropriate titles in the series.) Later they may turn to Richard Niebuhr's *Christ and Culture* (Harpers, now available in paperback), Dietrich Bonhoeffer's *The Cost of Discipleship* (Macmillan) or *Life Together* (Harpers), or Reinhold Niebuhr's *The Self and the Dramas of History* (Scribners). Or they may begin with a volume of the sermons of Paul Tillich, such as *The New Being* (Scribners) and move on to his *The Courage to Be* (Yale University Press).

Other groups might begin with a book on the Church, such as William McAfee Brown's *The Significance of the Church* (Layman's Theological Library, Westminster), or on a more advanced level, Claude Welch's *The Reality of the Church* (Scribners). A consideration might be given to the history of the Church, such as Dillenberger and Welch's *Protestant Christianity* (Scribners) or Martin E. Marty's *A Short History of Christianity* (Living Age Books). A book on the family might be studied, such as the elementary one of Hazen Werner, *Christian Family Living* (Basic Christian Books, Abingdon), or the more advanced, *Love and Conflict* by Gibson Winter (Doubleday). Other groups may be organized along occupational lines, using appropriate material to meet their specific problems.

Still other groups prefer to begin with the use of contemporary "secular" writings, whose number is legion. Those often used include Arthur Miller's play, *Death of a Salesman* (Bantam Books), Tennessee Williams' plays, such as *Cat on a Hot Tin Roof* (Signet), Albert Camus' works such as *The Stranger* (Vintage), William H. Whyte's *The Organization Man* (a Doubleday Anchor Book), or David Riesman's *The Lonely Crowd* (a Doubleday Anchor Book). Since almost all of these books, along with dozens of others, are in paperback editions, their purchase is not prohibitive.

Some groups will be ready to commence with depth Bible study; that is, the study of a book and its several passages in an attempt to understand both their original meaning and their

148

significance for us today. (I have sometimes been both disappointed and a little shocked at how difficult church people find such study, however.) One such method provides for groups of five or six to study together, first reading silently the passage under consideration. Each person may mark on a piece of paper the verses which bring some new insight by an exclamation mark, those where he has a question by question marks, and those which hit home by a cross mark. These insights and questions are then shared with one another as part of the process of clarification of the meaning of the passage.[14]

Another method suggests that each person rewrite the verses in his own language, sharing the revisions with the others and then facing up to the implications of taking the ideas seriously in life today.[15] In both cases it is necessary to divide a larger group into smaller ones, with perhaps some reporting from the smaller groups to the larger one.

Approaches to Study. In all of these samples some specific material is suggested for group consideration: a chapter in a book, an article, a play, a passage from the Bible, and so on. Previous reading is at least desirable if not mandatory. If such reading has not taken place, then the first part of the period must be spent in individual or group study. Or some person may read a paper or make a brief presentation, though this is an inadequate substitute for previous study. John Fry, after concluding his rather harsh criticism of the kind of ideas which have been presented in this chapter, suggests small group study in which the teacher is actually a book. "The life of the contract group," he asserts, "alternates between private reading and public testing at a pace predetermined by the end time."[16] The "testing" is the consideration which the group makes of the material being studied.

Procedure. Some method of getting the discussion under way is necessary. If the group is small and accustomed to studying together, someone may simply raise a question in order to get the group started, such a person having been asked in advance to do so. In a somewhat more formal setting, a brief summary may be useful. Using a painting, or photograph (such as those from the "Family of Man" series), may provoke the discussion. A simple dramatic situation played out by two or three members of the groups (role playing) might at times be useful, and occasionally an appropriate projected audio-visual material might be utilized. In larger groups, especially where discussion has not always begun easily, a committee may be asked to prepare in advance a brief presentation to begin the session. In a more formal seminar a paper prepared and read by a member may be necessary.

A resource person, if he does not dominate, can be helpful in introducing new material, raising questions, challenging conclusions too easily reached, and pointing to other facets of the problem. The availability of various printed resources is an asset.

The discussion leader in a more formal situation is responsible for seeing that the discussion is begun; that it does not wander too far away from the main concern; that all members of the group are encouraged to speak; and that no one person or small group dominates. Although in small and informal groups such a leader may not be required, in larger ones not accustomed to talking together he may be quite necessary.

In any case the "full and free discussion" which we have previously emphasized must be the rule. Either the leader or group members must be sensitive to those who are less likely to speak because of timidity. I have been in groups where the one remark made by the person who usually remained silent was the key to the session's meaning.

Most of us are impatient if conclusions are not obviously reached by a group, though this should not necessarily be the case. Neither agreement nor concensus is necessary, though often there *will* be a meeting of minds. A productive group may go no further than the clarification of issues, the sharing of

150

beliefs, the presentation of information, the raising of questions concerning answers which are too facile, and the challenging of prejudices. There may be a series of sessions together before any measurable results can be entered into the group's annals. Indeed, it is not "groupthink," to use William H. Whyte's picturesque phrase, with which such a group is concerned, but rather that each person may discover the will of God for his life.

In the process of study together, in which there is mutual respect and acceptance, genuine *koinonia* may emerge. Until this occurs the true depth of group life from the Christian perspective has not occurred. John Fry has made a very telling criticism of the obsession by adult Christian educators with "the person," insisting that "the person to them is an idealized portrait of all that modern man should be." [17] The easy manner in which we speak of personal groups ought to be challenged, but I am bold to make the following statement in spite of Fry's criticisms: This respect for one another as persons under God, in which each individual is treated as a *thou* (person), not an *it* (thing), is a prerequisite for the development of the Christian group. If this does not happen to some extent, then our groups have failed.

Duration of the Group. How long should a group continue? Fry answers the question arbitrarily by insisting that a study group should contract together for a stated length of time, at the termination of which the group is dissolved.[18] His fear of the development of group exclusiveness is a point well taken, but I think he carries it to extremes. Thus it seems impossible to me to answer the question categorically, for it should continue so long as its life together is productive. It ceases to be truly productive when it becomes so concerned for its own life as a group that it fails to reach out beyond itself. Because of the need for personal identity, which a small group can help supply, some risks must be taken by allowing groups to develop self-consciousness.

151

The answer which advocates of fellowship groups give to the question of duration is that new people ought to be introduced regularly into the group, and when it has reached twelve or fifteen in number it should then be divided into two groups. This procedure might be followed by study groups, with a new basis for study being selected at the time of division. The problem may be solved for other groups by population mobility, with new persons entering the group as others move away. Fry's suggestion of the contract, or terminal, group is another possibility, with new groups begun regularly on the basis of interest. In the case of groups that remain together indefinitely—as in the case of adult Sunday-school classes—there should be regular self-examination lest they become self-centered. Such groups should also seek means through which they can reach out beyond their own life to the total congregation and to the larger culture.

Although much that has been said in this chapter can be applied to all groups regardless of size and type, we have concluded by pointing to the need for small groups in a congregation in which serious study can be carried out and a sense of personal identity under God can be found. Such groups, we have noted, may begin in a variety of ways and follow many patterns. The danger of exclusiveness has been indicated and ways of encouraging a larger concern have been suggested. Certain risks must be taken, even that of a group's becoming ingrown.

This is not meant as a denial of other means by which the laity can be prepared for their work of ministry. Public lectures, panels and forums, and other ways in which significant contributions can be made to the intellectual life of the congregation should be utilized. Undergirding all of these is the life of worship of the congregation, the celebration of the sacraments, and the presentation of the word in preaching. In all these ways it is hoped that God may be able to break through man's weakness to manifest *his* judgment, love, and grace.

NOTES

1. Summaries of these developments will be found in the following books: Daniel Day Williams, *What Present-Day Theologians Are Thinking* (rev. ed.; New York: Harper & Brothers, 1959); William Hordern, *A Layman's Guide to Protestant Theology* (New York: The Macmillan Company, 1955); and *The Case for a New Reformation Theology* (Philadelphia: The Westminster Press, 1959).
2. Many books and articles have been published in this field during recent years, and the following are only suggestive. Brief summaries of the application of group development theory to Christian education will be found in David J. Ernsberger, *A Philosophy of Adult Christian Education* (Philadelphia: The Westminster Press, 1959) and C. Ellis Nelson, "Group Dynamics and Religious Education," in *Religious Education: A Comprehensive Survey*, ed. Marvin J. Taylor (Nashville: Abingdon Press, 1960). See also Paul Bergevin and John McKinley, *Design for Adult Education in the Church* (Greenwich, Conn.: The Seabury Press, 1958); Paul F. Douglass, *The Group Workshop Way in the Church* (New York: Association Press, 1956); Mary Alice Douty, *How to Work with Church Groups* (Nashville: Abingdon Press, 1957); and Sara Little, *Learning Together in the Christian Fellowship* (Richmond, Va.: John Knox Press, 1956). For more technical discussions, see *Group Dynamics: Research and Theory*, ed. Dorwin Cartwright and Alvin Zander (Evanston, Ill.: Row, Peterson and Company, 1953); Hubert Bonner, *Group Dynamics: Principles and Applications* (New York: The Ronald Press Company, 1959); and Murray G. Ross and Charles E. Hendry, *New Understandings of Leadership* (New York: Association Press, 1957).
3. "A Plain Account of the People Called Methodists," II.7, in *The Works of the Rev. John Wesley*, A. M. (London: John Mason, 1841), VIII, 244.
4. J. R. Kidd, *How Adults Learn* (New York: Association Press, 1959), p. 131. (Italics his.)
5. I have discussed church administration in *The Church Redemptive, op. cit.*, Chap. 11.
6. The dual role of the teacher in providing a "setting for learning" and "learning tasks" is suggested in a booklet from the Division of Christian Education of the National Council of Churches, *The Objective of Christian Education for Senior High Young People* (475 Riverside Drive, New York 27, New York, 1958), pp. 14-15, 32-38.
7. The various types of leadership necessary are discussed by A. A. Liveright, in *Strategies of Leadership: In Conducting Adult Education Programs* (New York: Harper & Brothers, 1959), especially Chap. 3.
8. See note 2 for suggestions at this point.
9. This distinction is made in a helpful chapter on the nature of church groups, "Christian Fellowship and Mental Health," in *The Church and*

Mental Health, ed. Paul B. Maves (New York: Charles Scribner's Sons, 1953), Chap. 3-A.

10. These and other methods are clearly described in John McKinley's *Creative Methods for Adult Classes* (St. Louis. The Bethany Press, 1960).

11. J. R. Kidd, for example, estimates that the number of adults in formal and informal education enterprises rose from fifteen million in 1924 to fifty million in 1955 (*Op. cit.*, p. 34). Although this number is higher than that sometimes given, the growth is impressive in any case.

12. See, for example, Casteel, *op. cit.*, Illustrations are given *supra*, Chap. 6.

13. Paul Tillich, *Systematic Theology*, I, 59-66 and *passim*.

14. This approach has received fairly wide acceptance, but I have not found a specific reference which describes it in detail.

15. Ross Snyder, "Depth and Encounter Study of the Bible" (a leaflet reprinted from *The High Call*, Spring, 1960). For a somewhat different approach, see E. H. Robertson, *'Take and Read': A Guide to Group Bible Study* (Naperville, Ill.: SCM Book Club, 1961), especially Chap. 1. Suzanne de Dietrich has done pioneer work in this approach to Bible study. An example is found in her recent *Free Men: Meditations on The Bible Today*, trans. and with an introduction by Olive Wyon (Naperville, Ill.: SCM Book Club, 1961).

16. From *A Hard Look at Christian Adult Education* by John R. Fry. © 1961, W. L. Jenkins. The Westminster Press. Used by permission.

17. *Ibid.*, p. 49.

18. *Ibid.*, pp. 122-24.

CHAPTER 8

TOWARD THE RENEWAL OF THE CHURCH

In the providence of God new forms of church life are emerging in our time—such forms as have been described in previous chapters. The forms themselves are relatively unimportant; the impulse which is bringing them into being is. They represent both man's search for meaning and direction and God's initiative in providing an answer to man's need. The Spirit is ever breaking through the traditions in which man seeks to contain the gospel. Man's organized religious expressions are continually in need of being transcended by the activity of God. God is the same and that which he is trying to say and do for man is that which he said and did in Jesus Christ. The Scriptures, as witness to the original events of revelation in Israel and especially in Jesus Christ, are the indispensable resources in giving form and direction to man's apprehension of the acts of God today. What is demanded, however, is not a slavish copying of biblical forms but the response of free men to the God who stands behind all forms. The heritage on which we build is crucial—but as guide, not as mold.

The Present Situation

This word concerning the necessity of radical change is imperative because the human situation to which the gospel must speak in our day is not one which encourages optimism. In the countries dominated by Communist ideology there is either open persecution or harassment of Christians. In those areas where new nations are rising, such religions as Islam, Hinduism, and Buddhism are often linked with national aspirations so that the Christian mission is seriously curtailed. Some of these faiths, having become again or for the first time militantly missionary, are even invading the so-called Christian West. In much of the West the Church is relatively ineffective, and where it is culturally respectable it has often so accommodated itself to the culture that it is scarcely identifiable from the culture. In the name of anticommunism rival faiths have arisen which seek to silence the voice of the Church and of concerned churchmen. The hope of the Student Volunteer Movement as this century was born, that the world might be won for Christ in that generation, appears now to have been an empty dream devoid of substance or realism.

Yet the situation which present-day Christians face is no more difficult and in the West not nearly so dangerous—as that which first-century Christians faced. During the early days, as the writings of Paul indicate, the Church could still trust in a reasonably friendly state, and thus Paul could enjoin his Roman readers to "be subject to the governing authorities" (Rom. 13:1). This condition did not persist for long, however; nor while it continued did it preclude discouragement, disappointment, seemingly insurmountable difficulties, and even persecution from local authorities. "Afflictions, hardships, calamities, beatings, imprisonments, tumults, labors, watching, hunger" comprise one of Paul's list of descriptive characteristics of his life as an apostle (II Cor. 6:4-5; see also II Cor. 11:24-28). Yet he could also write:

We are afflicted in every way, but not crushed; perplexed, but not driven to despair; persecuted, but not forsaken; struck down, but not destroyed. . . . So we do not lose heart. Though our outer nature is wasting away, our inner nature is being renewed every day. For this slight momentary affliction is preparing for us an eternal weight of glory beyond all comparison, because we look not to the things that are seen but to the things that are unseen; for the things that are seen are transient, but the things that are unseen are eternal.

—II Cor. 4:8-9, 16-18

This understanding of the Christian gospel is a far cry from the "peace of mind" religion-in-general which characterizes much of American Protestantism today. It is miles away from the easy religion which is popular in suburbia where Protestantism is flourishing. Gibson Winter, to whom we have previously referred, calls this phenomenon the "suburban captivity of the churches" [1] and describes "the new religious style" as consisting of the organizational church with its many organizations and activities, concluding that such a church has become "introverted." He goes on to say:

The introverted church is one which puts its own survival before its mission, its own identity above its task, its internal concerns before its apostolate, its rituals before its ministry. These contrasts distinguish the Church as a structure and the Church a living power—its static and dynamic aspects. . . . Undue emphasis on the static structure of the Church has led to the disappearance of a significant lay ministry in denominational Protestantism. Loss of dynamic form and surrender of mission undercut the lay ministry, for it is the Church as mission which rests its case upon the laity and their outreach to the world.[2]

Sufficient evidence has been presented in previous chapters to indicate that this is not the full story of modern Protestantism, though it is far too common for us to be complacent about it. Nor is this criticism of the overorganized and over-institutionalized denomination a denial of the necessity of

157

both the institutional aspects of Christianity and organization. Administration of the life of the Church has been a part of its work since before the first deacons were chosen in order to relieve the apostles from many of the administrative details which had arisen (Acts 6:1-6).

The crucial question for Protestantism with respect to organization is whether the new zeal which is emerging within both clergy and laity, the new forms and structures which are arising, the new understanding of the meaning of the Gospel which are needed in the modern world will emerge as a dominant force or be crushed under the weight of the organizational church. If Winter is in any sense right, we are always in danger of the latter, and if we are sufficiently introverted—as he thinks we are—we may never be conscious of what is happening since we will be doing it, supposedly, in the name of the gospel!

God will not be defeated, of course, but it may be necessary for him to go outside the organized church for the message of reconciling love to be heard and experienced. Our primary concern, to be sure, is not whether Protestantism will survive or perish; but as Protestant Christians we ought to be mightily concerned whether we are acting responsibly both through the existing structures of church life as well as by bringing into being new ones through which the Spirit of the Christ may be made known.

We either are living at the end of the Protestant era— or at the beginning of a new era in the Church. These pages are written just after the meeting of the third assembly of the World Council of Churches at New Delhi which some observers interpret as the most significant single meeting of the Church since the Protestant Reformation. We cannot know whether this is true or not. In any case it is what happens as a result of such a meeting that finally will tell the story, and the crucial question, as it was in the first centuries of the Church, is whether or not individual Christians will be sufficiently stirred by the Spirit of God to respond meaningfully to the challenge of the world's need for meaning and salvation. And so we must, in these final pages, speak of the importance of the individual Christian, the laity in particular but also the clergy and other full-time church workers, if the Church is to fulfill its mission and task in the twentieth century.

The Necessity of Commitment

The major concern of these chapters has been either directly or indirectly the rebirth of the laity; and rebirth has been used in a dual manner. The more obvious meaning refers to the rebirth of a lay emphasis in the organized church; that is, the reassertion of the New Testament doctrine of the Church as the whole people of God, not a company of persons of a secondary order presided over by a primary order of clerics and professionals. This type of rebirth is impossible, however, without a deeper kind; namely, the rebirth of the laity in terms of commitment, concern, and mission. Those who fear a lay-centered Church can point with justifiable questions to lay groups which have arisen within the last fifteen years whose interest is to thwart the Church in its fight against racial segregation, social and economic injustice, and other matters of Christian concern. The indiscriminate criticism of clergy-men as being Communist sympathizers often represents either a conscious or unconscious attempt to discredit the Church when it seeks to make the gospel relevant to the issues of the modern world, and thus points to a lack of basic commitment to that for which the Church stands.

What is required if both clergy and laity are to be the Body of Christ in the world is a renewed and deepened personal and corporate commitment to the gospel, and this means essentially an active, informed dedication to the proposition that God in Christ brings meaning and hope to a distraught and divided world. The message committee of the New Delhi

159

meeting of the World Council of Churches put this cogently
in these words:

When we speak to men as Christians we must speak the truth
of our faith: that there is only one way to the Father, namely Jesus
Christ, His Son. On that one way we are bound to meet our
brother. We meet our brother Christian. We meet also our brother
man; and before we speak to him of Christ, Christ has already
sought him.[3]

Much that divides us as Christians today comes about because the foundational character of this basic commitment is
forgotten. We are too concerned with belief *about* rather than
belief *in*, or commitment *to*. For example, a storm of protest
arose not long ago upon the publication of Schubert Ogden's
Christ Without Myth, which questioned many of the traditional ways of describing who Jesus Christ is and how he becomes meaningful to men today. Theological argument is
good; indeed this is part of the ferment in which we are now
engaged as we seek to make the gospel relevant to contemporary life. Unfortunately, however, this discussion was carried
on at the level of heresy hunting; that is, with relation to beliefs
about Jesus Christ. Never once did those who saw in the statements a challenge to traditional ways of speaking about Christ
ask the question, "Is this writer really committed to Christ as
the key to the meaning of existence?" Actually the purpose of
the book was to assert, in terms different from those we normally use, precisely this reality. Those who raised the questions
were thus participants in a new scholasticism; that is, a concern
that our beliefs be stated in a particular way, not that our lives
be oriented in a particular direction.

I do not mean to deny the importance of theological discussion—in fact, quite the contrary, as the preceding chapters
indicate. Zeal without knowledge is a dangerous thing, and
part of the misplaced lay criticism of the Church is due to

inadequate knowledge of what the gospel is. The problem in theological thinking arises, however, whether it is engaged in by relatively untutored laymen or by sophisticated theologians, when theology is substituted for faith and commitment rather than being considered a reflection on faith and commitment.

Or, as Elton Trueblood has reminded us, we begin to bog down in our Christian living when we substitute belief *about* (or *that*) for belief *in*. This is the difference between cognitive knowledge (knowledge *about*) and existential knowledge (knowledge *of* and response *to*). As Trueblood puts it:

A Christian is a person who confesses that, amidst the manifold and confusing voices heard in the world, there is one Voice which supremely wins his full assent, uniting all his powers, intellectual and emotional, into a single pattern of self-giving. That Voice is Jesus Christ. A Christian not only believes *that* He was; he believes *in Him* with all his heart and strength and mind. Christ appears to the Christian as the one stable point or fulcrum in all the relativities of history. Once the Christian has made this primary commitment he still has perplexities, but he begins to know the joy of being used for a mighty purpose, by which his little life is dignified.[4]

But how, you may ask, does a person go about choosing that to which he will be committed, and how does he lead others to commitment? We must admit at the outset that faith is in one sense a gift—"For by grace you have been saved through faith; and this is not your own doing, it is the gift of God." (Eph. 2:8). If you have ever tried to conjure up faith or a sense of commitment—for the two are very close to each other—in any thing or in any person, you know how ineffective proofs of the worthiness of the desired object of faith are. This is why "proofs of the existence of God" are not likely to convince the atheist, nor are rational—or irrational—explanations of the reality of Jesus Christ likely to convince the nonbeliever. Rather, we are committed to a cause in which

161

we are "caught up"; we have faith in that which grasps us because it points to meaning where none has appeared to be. Thus nationalism has become the faith of many of the rising people of the world, even when there is not much rational basis for such nationalism; and superpatriotism has become the faith of many Americans because the Christian faith no longer provides meaning for them and they are caught up in a wave of fear which leads to hysteria.

So it is with our commitment to Christ, or the commitment of those to whom we witness. We must be "caught up" into a community of faith, a community which may consist of only two or three people or of a much larger group. Trueblood is right when he insists that commitment cannot be dissociated from the Church.[5] By placing ourselves in situations where at least some degree of faith is present we too may become recipients of faith. So as we are concerned with the spread of our faith we must begin with the Church, however fumbling and inadequate it may be. It may be, in fact, only a remnant in any congregation who are faithful men, and faith at its best is a precarious thing in a world of so many rival faiths. But there is no other place to begin.

Thus it may be in a particular congregation only a small group into whose fellowship others may be drawn. Douglas Blatherwick, a British Methodist layman, has described what may happen in this way: "It may mean only two or three meeting with the minister. If there are no lay spiritual leaders it may mean that the minister will prepare and pray and pray and pray until some human barrier is broken down."[6] Tom Allan, a British clergyman, has described how it was a "small and inarticulate group of people" in his congregation which began the process which led to radical transformation.[7] In a church in Texas where the pastor was told that if something did not happen soon the congregation would be abandoned, it was the pastor's course in biblical theology which began the process of change. (Within less than ten years a new building had been built for the congregation!) [8] For Robert Raines it was the plea of one couple that they knew nothing about their faith which led to his drawing together a small group for study and prayer.[9] And so the story runs—not very spectacular, but over and over again indicating that a deepened commitment is possible, that the rebirth of the laity is not only imminent but actually here.

The Possibility of Reconciliation

If commitment is a necessity for the renewal of the Church, reconciliation is the reality which can make commitment possible. As adequate a summary of the gospel as John 3:16 is II Cor. 5:19: "God was in Christ reconciling the world to himself." Reconciliation is essentially the bringing of man to the place where he is himself and where he is in right relationship with God and neighbor. It is the healing of broken relationships and the restoration of the image of God in man.

The accompanying injunctions in the same chapter are equally apt as a statement of the Christian's vocation: We are entrusted with "the ministry of reconciliation"—"We are ambassadors for Christ, God making his appeal through us" (II Cor. 5:18, 20). Here is a double-barreled possibility, then: it is through our being drawn into Christian fellowship that we may experience God's reconciling love, and we in turn may then become agents of reconciliation.[10] To be sure, we must heed the fear of John Fry that the emphasis on the group life of the church will become a new idolatry, not moving beyond the area of *human* association. After indicating the possibility of libidinous (that is, sexual) aspects of such small groups, he concludes: "Their discussion of the gospel . . . has a kind of private—'for us only'—tone. The world with its monster-like problems is dyked out." [11] Yet in our depersonalized society, the possibility of receiving God's reconciling love is more likely to materialize as persons are drawn into a group or into

163

a personal relationship where some degree of reconciliation, at least on a human level, is a reality. If it stops short of concern for the neighbor beyond the group, then Fry is right: it has failed to become a medium for receiving God's reconciliation.

The individual in our society is in search of groups in which he can find personal identity and meaning, and often the structured groups prove inadequate to meet these needs because they too are impersonal. The gang is an example of the unstructured personal group for teen-agers; the group which meets around the high altar of the swimming pool in a Hollywood-type apartment house is one form which it takes for single young adults. For the middle class, the family often serves the function—though not always—but in all strata of society there is a searching for something which brings personal identity.

To assert the possibility that reconciliation can become a reality in personal and group relationships is not to deny the importance of preaching, worship, and the sacraments as means of grace. Indeed, human association apart from the life of worship and the sacraments is likely to fall into the errors to which Mr. Fry points. On the other hand, all of us need the fellowship of the committed to strengthen whatever commitment has become ours, and there are many who refuse to participate in the Church's life of worship or even to come into its building for group relationships. Hence, it is often through the laity in dispersion that the experience of personal relationship must be found if it is to be Christian in quality. Arnold Come, after commenting on II Cor. 3:3 ("You are a letter from Christ delivered by us, written not with ink but with the Spirit of the living God, not on tablets of stone but on tablets of human hearts") concludes:

The startling and momentous implication follows, therefore, that Paul conceived of God's new covenant of reconciliation of the whole world as being ministered (mediated), not through the preaching of the Word and the administration of the sacraments within the church, but through the active wordless witness of the whole Christian community in its dynamic living relationship with all the world.[13]

The Disciplined Life

For the person who has responded to God's reconciling love in faith and commitment, there is the need for instruction that informs him of the nature of that commitment, and discipline which keeps him aware of who he is and what his mission must be. Christian teaching, as we have implied in sections dealing with adult study groups, consists of two major aspects: the introduction of the person into Christian community and instruction of him in the meaning of the faith. These are not discrete steps, of course, nor are they always followed in the same order. Instruction of some kind may precede introduction into genuine community, and preaching alone may awaken faith which then finds form and substance in the disciplined learning group. Further, the settled Christian still has need for the support of the corporate life of the intentional group as well as the larger congregation. In other words, he needs the disciplines of both personal and corporate Christian practices.

Generally speaking, Protestants have feared exterior means of attesting to and supporting one's faith, rightly fearing the church which controls the life of its members. Increasingly within recent years, however, many have rediscovered the necessity of voluntarily assuming certain disciplines which serve both as expression of one's faith and, at the same time, as means of strengthening faith. The fact that the old-line denominations in America have tended to become "established churches" has tended toward the same kind of easy church membership which characterizes the established state church. As Robert Raines has put it: "We of the liberal Protestant tradition have accommodated ourselves to the

165

cultural climate of the free and easy." [13] Whether or not it is feasible to introduce into the requirements for general church membership at least minimal standards of discipline cannot be discussed at this point; it does seem obvious, however, that both clergy and laity who desire to be more than nominal Christians need to reassess the place that regular, stated "habits of holy living" have in the life of the modern Christian.

One way in which this is being done is through the disciplined group, in which members assume agreed-upon habits of the community. For such a community as Taizé in southern France, this involves permanent and resident membership in a community that is similar to the monastic group, with the disciplines of celibacy, community of goods, and obedience. For members of the Iona Community in Scotland, the discipline of community living involves only one week each year at the Abbey, with other disciplines practiced in the life of the parish (for clergy members) and in the life of the world (for lay members). The East Harlem Protestant Parish in New York City has set up seven disciplines with only slight variations for those on the team ministry of the parish from other members. These involve the ordered day, including prayer but also a disciplined way of spending the entire day; regular participation in worship and the sacrament of Holy Communion; weekly participation in an "enabling group" with fellow Christians, Bible study, for example; discussion once a month with a selected friend concerning the progress of one's Christian life; regularly giving of income; participation in at least one community organization working for justice or brotherhood; and the faithful exercise of one's ministry on behalf of the congregation.[14]

Raines suggests the possibility that small groups within the congregation may follow such disciplines, six of which he lists: corporate worship, daily prayer, Bible reading and study, the giving of money, service, and witness. The first three, he notes, are means by which we open ourselves to the grace of God; the last three, means by which we share the grace given to us.[15] Even when no such group disciplines are available, each person may set up on his own individual disciplines, with the following areas especially crucial: (a) the discipline of regular participation in worship and Holy Communion; (b) the discipline of private prayer; (c) the discipline of group study of the Christian faith; and (d) the discipline of service, including the giving of a portion of one's income for the Church and charitable purposes, the performing of some kind of service in the name of the Church, and the engagement in community projects concerned with human welfare and the improvement of society. A part of one's service ought, of course, to be witness, but this seems to me to grow out of the disciplined life and to be related to it in its entirety. The person who has ordered his life according to the gospel will naturally find the forms and structures through which his witness can be made.

A special word may be said about the importance of corporate worship as part of the disciplined life. Protestants have often thought of worship, including participation in Holy Communion, as being something which they do or fail to do depending upon how they feel about what goes on in the corporate act. Thus the picture of worship which is presented tends to be one in which the worshiper is a spectator, not a participant. Yet as has been repeatedly shown liturgy, "the ordering of the act of worship," is not something said but something done;[16] that is, it is not just ritual but rather a mode of action in which celebrant and people together offer themselves corporately before God in thanksgiving, praise, confession, receptivity, and commitment.

To be sure, Protestant worship probably fails as often as Roman Catholic worship does in being truly a corporate act, a celebration by all worshipers together; and the "liturgical revival," when understood in its true meaning, is an effort to restore Christian worship to its original form in which

167

there were no passive onlookers but only active worshipers. Precisely how this is done is not the question to be discussed here; it may be in quite conventional ways, using the historic forms of worship, or it may be in rather unconventional ways, such as George Webber has described in connection with the East Harlem Protestant Parish.[17] I am less concerned now than I once was as to whether we recover historic forms. Indeed, I am not sure that this is necessarily a good thing, for they may be hindrances to meaningful worship. And though one ought to participate in public worship as part of the disciplined life whether he "gets anything out of it or not," nevertheless it is to be hoped that it will become for him an effective means of grace.

The Recovery of Mission

All along, both in this chapter and in previous ones, we have pointed to the crucial task of the Church as being the recovery of mission and the rediscovery of its ministry. We have looked both at the inner mission of the Church (that is, the carrying on of its interior life) and the mission to the world. Some contemporary writers appear to deny too easily the importance of the first of these ministries, seeming to ignore the significance of the daily round of duties performed as part of the structured life of the congregation. To be sure, the almost exclusive emphasis in popular thought on the mission of the Church inside its walls must be offset by a strong statement of the necessity of the larger mission. And this mission to the world, as we have repeatedly said, is almost exclusively the work of the laity.

While the Church's ministry in the world must be carried out primarily by laymen, the clergy and other full-time workers in the Church bear a particular responsibility in challenging the laity to greater concern, in instructing them in the meaning of the Word, and in guiding them to responsible action.

168

If the clergyman's chief responsibility is, as the ordination rituals often say, to dispense the Word of God and the sacraments, then he is in a particularly responsible position with respect to the total ministry of the Church. Although he cannot carry out this ministry alone—as he may be tempted to do—he must, along with others of the set-apart ministry, be one through whom the impulse for ministry is encouraged and stimulated.

This special emphasis on the set-apart ministry does not mean that the thesis upon which these chapters have been based has been abandoned. It is simply to assert that, by virtue of the special preparation of set-apart ministers, their greater freedom to approach the life of the Church creatively and imaginatively, their responsibilities as office-bearers which have either historic or current emphases in the Church, they are more likely to be the key to renewal in a congregation. These special ministers are basically not different from the other laity, for all have received the same call, to be faithful disciples of Jesus Christ. This special responsibility arises because the Church has set them apart for special ministries and has provided for them preparation which makes them presumably more able to be the key person in an imaginative approach to making the gospel meaningful to those both inside and outside the Church.

Let us repeat—it is the whole people who must all together carry out the mission of the Church. But will laymen respond when these greater demands are laid upon them? We can say categorically that not all will do so, as even now not all do so in regard to the inner life of the congregation. Yet I am repeatedly amazed at the faithfulness of laymen in carrying on the activities of the Church, even though they are often misdirected, and equally so at how eagerly at least some respond to a deeper understanding of their Christian responsibility. Enough examples have been given in earlier chapters to indicate the truth of this statement, and they could be multiplied many times even in my limited experience and much more so in the experience of others. We dare not be so presumptuous as to say that a real revival in the Church is occurring, but there are enough evidences of it that we can at least hope that such is the case.

This rebirth of the laity—both in the sense of a reassertion of the wholeness of the Church and in respect to the lives of individual laymen—is one of the signs of hope in the Church. To be sure, the forces both within and outside the Church which seek to crush this heightened concern are formidable. We are always in danger that the organization church will defeat the Church of Jesus Christ even though we cannot do without organization. These comments are not intended to be a call either to clergymen or to laymen to become rebels against the institution: most of us are not cut out to be reformers—if indeed anyone is. Only God can in the final analysis reform the Church. But we are called to act responsibly even in the face of difficulties. Whatever else the clergy must do in our time, they must call the laity to responsible action as Christian disciples both in the Church and in the world.

We cannot predict how fully God will be able to work among us his work of grace. It is our responsibility only to plant and water, to be faithful in our response to the demands of the gospel. God must give the growth, but "we are fellow workers in God's service." [18] In this service we—both clergy and laity, but especially the laity—are sent into the world God loves to be his agents of reconciliation.

NOTES

1. Winter, op. cit.
2. Ibid., p. 103.
3. "Ecumenical Press Service," 28th Year, No. 48, December 8, 1961.
4. Elton Trueblood, The Company of the Committed (New York: Harper & Brothers, 1961), p. 23.

5. *Ibid.*, especially p. 21.
6. Blatherwick, *op. cit.*, p. 91.
7. Tom Allan, *The Face of My Parish* (London: Student Christian Movement Press, 1954), pp. 68-70.
8. McKinley Avenue Methodist Church, San Antonio, Texas, The Rev. Claus Rohlfs, Pastor.
9. Raines, *op. cit.*, p. 84.
10. This is the particular emphasis of Come's *Agents of Reconciliation.*
11. Fry, *op. cit.*, p. 26.
12. Come, *op. cit.*, pp. 154-55.
13. Raines, *op. cit.*, p. 56.
14. *God's Colony in Man's World, op. cit.*, pp. 139-43.
15. Raines, *op. cit.*, pp. 59-63; 99-100.
16. See, for example, Dix, *op. cit.*, especially Chaps. 1 and 11. I have discussed the matter in *The Church Redemptive, op. cit.*, Chap. 6.
17. "Worship in East Harlem," *Union Seminary Quarterly Review*, XVII (Jan. 1962) 143-51.
18. The alternative reading for I Cor. 3:9a in *The New English Bible, op cit.*, p. 283.

INDEX

Date Due